Paradoxes in Lacanian Psychoanalysis

This book explores the nature of paradoxes in Lacanian psychoanalysis, how they can be approached in treatment and how they can be resolved.

Building on Freud's and Lacan's own work in resolving paradoxes, Yehuda Israely considers psychic distress, and its amelioration, by means of the study and clarification of the many life situations that can be described as paradoxical. Among the paradoxes examined in this book are the nature of longing (the object's presence in its absence), the wholeness of the broken heart (the subject's existence in relation to the lack that defines her or him), drives (the more you feed it, the hungrier it gets) and the pangs of conscience (the righteous suffer). Israely's innovative approach considers several questions which can be used to orient treatment and focuses on shedding the erroneous beliefs and assumptions that can lead to dead ends. *Paradoxes in Lacanian Psychoanalysis* also explores those paradoxes – involving anxiety, perplexity, wonder and creativity – that cannot and are not meant to be resolved.

This fascinating book will be essential reading for Lacanian psychoanalysts in practice and in training, and for psychoanalysts and psychotherapists of other theoretical backgrounds who are interested in understanding the nature of paradoxes.

Yehuda Israely is a clinical psychologist, psychoanalyst and author based in Israel. He is Director of the Moebius Institute in Tel-Aviv, member of the Tel-Aviv Forum of the International Forums of the Lacanian Field and his previous publications include *Lacanian Treatment: Psychoanalysis for Clinicians* (Routledge).

"Characterized by exceptional clarity of thought, this book by Israely is yet another considerable contribution to the Lacanian discourse. Employing philosophical and physical principles, Israely clarifies the logic supporting the analytic cure in its dissolution of various forms of suffering. This book is sure to captivate analysts, patients and analyzants."

– **Ofra Shalev**, psychoanalyst, Forum Lacan Tel-Aviv

Paradoxes in Lacanian Psychoanalysis

Yehuda Israely
Edited by Idan Oren
Translated by Mirjam Hadar

Routledge
Taylor & Francis Group

LONDON AND NEW YORK

Cover image: Gwoeii | Shutterstock.com

First published in English 2022
by Routledge
2 Park Square, Milton Park, Abingdon, Oxon OX14 4RN

and by Routledge
605 Third Avenue, New York, NY 10158

Routledge is an imprint of the Taylor & Francis Group, an informa business

© 2022 Yehuda Israely

Translated by Mirjam Hadar

The right of Yehuda Israely to be identified as author of this work has been asserted in accordance with sections 77 and 78 of the Copyright, Designs and Patents Act 1988.

Published in Hebrew by Resling 2020

British Library Cataloguing-in-Publication Data
A catalogue record for this book is available from the British Library

Library of Congress Cataloging-in-Publication Data
A catalog record has been requested for this book

ISBN: 9781032140834 (hbk)
ISBN: 9781032140841 (pbk)
ISBN: 9781003232285 (ebk)

DOI: 10.4324/9781003232285

Typeset in Bembo
by Apex CoVantage, LLC

Contents

Figures

Introduction

Paradox as a contradiction due to a mistaken assumption

Yehuda Israely

Psychoanalysis came into being as an attempt to solve a paradox. While Freud's neurology colleagues were dismissive of their patients who suffered from what they considered sham sensory or motor paralyses, he believed them (Freud, 2001 [1895]). In so doing, he agreed to accommodate the tension of holding two clashing truths at one and the same time, without having to reject one of them. He observed that these patients were suffering from paralysis, and yet as a physician he knew very well that there was no neurological impairment. "Glove anesthesia" was one such phenomenon. Here the patient suffers from a motor or sensory paralysis in roughly the area a glove usually covers. Since, however, the nerve runs along the limb, paralysis beginning at the end of the nerve's trajectory, from the wrist down, is impossible. Freud liked to believe that there were data concealed from both patients and physicians alike: if only he would uncover these, that would undo the paradox. He was right. The third truth, which clarifies the noncontradiction between the two clashing observations, appears when we assume what Freud called the unconscious. If we take it that the human psyche is split between a conscious and an unconscious part, then the symptom does not necessarily deceive. Indeed, the symptom points at a censored truth. On this assumption, Freud was able to refer to the symptom as not merely speaking but telling a truth. To solve the paradox, Freud had to invent the unconscious, and by doing so, he gave rise to psychoanalysis. Like him, psychoanalysts ever since have had to wait anxiously, perplexed, their attention floating, as they refrain from rushing into simplistic interpretations. Like him, they have had to wait for additional information that the unconscious will provide in dreams, slips and other expressions of the unconscious, to clarify what it was they observed and which basic assumptions they failed to note.

In this book, the concept of paradox I use is taken from the domain of logic, which studies the congruence between assumptions, or premises, and their outcomes. Where there is such congruence, a premise is true, and conversely, where there isn't congruence, then it must be false. Now, when we find both congruence and incongruence, then what we have is a paradox. In this book,

DOI: 10.4324/9781003232285-01

I will therefore recruit the logic of paradox and its solution to approach and resolve patients' afflictions. Formulating these afflictions in terms of paradox will enable us to resolve them as we would in the case of paradoxes. We will be guided in this by Freud's principle as it is reflected in his question of what is the hidden element. This would be the element which, once we disclose it, shows that the apparent contradiction behind the paradox is resolved. If paradox manifests itself as affliction or distress, then solving the former is bound to alleviate the latter.

Here is a classical paradox: if all humans are mortal, then Socrates, who is a human being, is mortal too. But if we said that all humans are mortals, yet the human being Socrates is immortal, we would encounter a paradox. For going by our own premises, he cannot be both a human being and immortal. If, however we consider the fact that it was we, ourselves, who made up the rules according to which these statements are made, then what we have is a kind of setup: paradox here features as a contradiction between statements of our own making. Paradox, in other words, can only emerge where we have statements that can be either confirmed or rejected: it does not occur in the actual, or real, world, only in the world that is constituted by statements. There is a paradox in the statement "A unicorn with two horns" because the statement flouts the premise defining "a unicorn", when in fact unicorns don't exist in the real world. The solution is therefore a conceptual one, requiring a change in our basic assumptions.

Wittgenstein considered reality a language game. This enabled him to solve paradoxes by dissolving their underlying assumptions. He claimed that problems don't get solved but dissolved (Wittgenstein, 2009). The reality in which we perceive a problem – or a paradox for that matter – is only one possible language game. If we move to another language game, the problem or paradox is likely to vanish. The solution of a paradox, in other words, is really by undoing it as a paradox. We don't need to be able to assume that it is somehow possible for a dead Socrates to be alive.

All it takes to see that there need be no contradiction is to widen the lens a little; then there is no clash between for instance the statement that Socrates has been dead for thousands of years in the biological meaning of that word, while in terms of his impact on Western philosophy, his spirit is still alive and kicking.

The well-known paradox of the liar illustrates how an erroneous premise results in paradox: When the liar announces "I am lying", does he speak the truth or is he lying? If it is the truth he's telling, then his being a liar stands confirmed; if what he says is a lie, then we must conclude that he is speaking the truth.

Had, instead, his statement been "You're lying" – the question of paradox would not have arisen. It may very well be true when he says about another person that he, that other person, is lying.

Figure 0.1 I am lying
Source: Original drawing by the author

Figure 0.2 You are lying
Source: Original drawing by the author

What is the shutter-minded premise that causes the paradox? And what must we bring into our field of vision so that the paradox may vanish? The misleading assumption is that the speaker in the first, paradoxical statement, represented by the drawing, is *one and the same person*, as the "I" in the spoken statement, in contrast with the speaker in the second, non-paradoxical statement, who is very clearly *not the same* as the one about whom he states that he is a liar. So, the solution to the paradox lies in us making the distinction between the speaker – who says the sentence "I am lying" – and the word "I", as it appears in the sentence "I am lying". Had the speaker formulated his statement as follows: "I am telling the truth right now when I say that I usually lie", the paradox would have vanished. The "I" of "right now" is not the same "I" of "usually".

Here is how paradox manifests itself through hysterical conversion: a patient does not manage to stand on his feet, though both the orthopedic surgeon and the neurologist have excluded organic causes. He tries to stand but he falls. At night, when he gets up to the toilet, half-asleep, he does not fall. This suggests an enactment of falling. The patient had in fact dropped out of a training program. His official version is that he wasn't at all sorry about it. The unofficial, unconscious version seems to be that his dropping out expresses itself (unconsciously) in collapsing again and again. Here the paradox is that while he is indifferent to having been unable to continue the training program, he suffers from it *at the same time*. It is only when we treat these falls as symptomatic that we can resolve this paradox; we can do this because there is no contradiction between the unperturbed position and the aggrieved one, once we think that these positions are held by two distinct functions: the conscious and the unconscious. In so far as it simultaneously represses and expresses the unconscious, the symptom is paradoxical. A symptom appears when the conscious ideal and the unconscious desire are in conflict. It exists only when we do not distinguish between the conscious and the unconscious position.

When a symptom presents itself, its solution will depend on both the analyst's and the patient's willingness to see it as one. It is, in other words, only possible to start wondering what it means, and eventually offer an interpretation, provided we perceive a symptom as such. If either the analyst or the patient – or both, and each for their own reason – choose not to investigate the symptom and examine what caused it – then the symptom will continue as before. Knowing that there is something to know doesn't mean choosing to know. This makes a certain sense from the patient's perspective: had he been willing to know, he would not have had to produce the symptom in the first place. Interpreting the symptom as "a downfall" or a "dropping-out", we were inviting the patient to make his grief conscious, that is, to undo the contradiction and thereby make the symptom, which represented the grief, unnecessary.

Like the paradox of the liar, the paradox of hysterical conversion Freud countenanced is clarified once we recognize the presence of splitting. In the former case, the splitting occurs between speaker and the object of speech; in the latter, it involves the distinction between conscious and unconscious. The person with hysterical conversion speaks the truth *in the conscious* when he reports that his hand is paralyzed, and another truth is interpreted by the analyst as spoken by *the unconscious* insofar as we can take the message – also – to be that his hand is not paralyzed. The statement of the unconscious is that the paralysis of his hand is a metaphor for such repressed drives. So, we can think of paradox as a riddle, which takes the following general shape: What is the invisible thing that will make it clear to us that paradox, here, is not inevitable? The answer is the split between the conscious and the unconscious.

The change in – or removal of – basic assumptions this involves can be compared to the experience of awakening: when we wake up, we shed the assumption that what we were just dreaming was real. The information which the dreamer misses as long as she is asleep becomes manifest as soon as she wakes up. In this sense, a paradox is resolved much in the same way as we wake up from a dream. If it's a nightmare, we feel very relieved, like with a painful symptom. Paradox is based in illusion. When we wake up from it, it disappears. It is no coincidence that in all mystical or spiritual traditions, personal growth takes the form of an awakening or an opening of the eyes. Meditation, for instance, is often described as an awakening from the dream of reality.

Like a Wittgensteinian approach, a Lacanian perspective has a clear advantage over positivist approaches. Because the former – which takes the concept of reality to be mythical in nature, a narrative made up from figures and images – is radically anti-essentialist, it enables an awakening from realities as given. This object is called a table because we have agreed to call it so. If we were employed in a furniture shop, we might have called it merchandise. Every narrative which goes by the name of "reality" comes to support a wishful way of seeing ourselves and the world. If we take the idea that paradox implies a mistake in our underlying assumptions, usually to the effect of losing sight of the larger picture, and if we venture further that healing the pain of the symptom requires setting this mistake straight, then we must ask where the mistake originates.

What causes an error to be a Freudian error is that it is not innocent; it is the outcome rather of an unconsciously motivated blindness to disregard the full, or fuller, picture. Here what it takes to wake from the dream or shed the illusion is for the subject of the unconscious to agree to let go of the intended blindness. The interpretation will function as an invitation to look at the evaded knowledge. The patient will unconsciously choose or agree whether to listen. Such agreement will be one step in the direction of healing: once the patient is conscious of the fact that she ignores the fuller picture, her field of vision will expand. It is due to the patient's own limited view that error happens: it allows her to cling to a story that depicts a reality full of flattering, reassuring, exciting or pleasing interpretations based on her basic assumptions. Many manners of distress and symptoms are the outcome of these paradoxical conditions. The analyst's interpretation comes to show what the narrative leaves out, an exclusion that results in the symptom. Translating distress into paradox is not a trivial task. Often, it is hard to discern which elements are the ones that will expand the picture. By far, the most difficult though is to get the patient to realize the virtual nature of her reality: after all, gaining such a perspective will require her to let go of a desire or pleasure which the narrative keeps intact as long as she considers it a necessary narrative.

Albert Einstein believed that the paradoxes in quantum theory were the result of the limited capacities of measurement instruments. Niels Bohr, by contrast, thought that chaos is inherent to the universe on the subatomic (i.e., quantum) level (Kumar, 2011). Einstein might have been in thrall to a Freudian error: a refusal to surrender the fantasy of a harmonious universe. A letter he wrote to Freud seems to support this, because there he complains about the lack of harmony among the nations (Freud & Einstein, 2001 [1933]). Freud's reply is level-headed and resembles his stance in *Totem and Taboo* (Freud, 2001 [1912–13], p. IX), where he claims it is only when the sons or brothers join hands that the dictator, who wallows in his unlimited pleasures, can be vanquished. Freud adds that a harmonious reality is not something we should hope for.

Expanding perspectives is not always beneficial as is the case with symptoms. For example, the persistent knowledge that our loved ones may die before us is not beneficial. It can become a true, yet obsessive thought. It is also important to state that not every distress or discontent is fixed by solving the paradox that supports it. There is a moment, in treatment as in life, when we must admit that paradox is inherent to life. We can expand our view up to a point, and we can add only so many dimensions. There's a limit to our ability to apply symbolic logic to real paradoxical phenomena.

In this book I will be looking at some of the key coordinates of Lacanian psychoanalysis through the notion of paradox. For each of the paradoxes I examine, I will clarify the associated theoretical psychoanalytical concepts, illustrate the psychic problems it generates and propose interpretations and clinical interventions. These interventions come to expose the patient to the possibility of dealing with his distress by formulating it in terms of paradox. This will set him on a search for missing information or a perspective not taken and lead to a solution as he rejects earlier assumptions which fed into the paradox. Here are the main paradoxes which the following chapters will discuss:

1   The object vs existence paradox – the object exists in its absence, that is, it must be absent to exist; or in other words, the existence of the object relies on its distinction from its background, a distinction that requires the possibility of its disappearance.
2   The paradox of becoming – "There's nothing more whole than a broken heart"; the human subject exists due to what they lack. There are subsections to this paradox, all of which point at different modes of subjecthood: (a) The paradox of subject in relation to object; we can formulate the paradoxical relations between object and subject in terms of the joke about the masochist asking the sadist to flog him: with typical sadistic pleasure, the sadist refuses. This response is both gratifying and frustrating at the same time. This double inversion is typical of humans because it is embedded in symbolic language, which uniquely allows for paradoxes like "I feel really satisfied to feel hungry at last". (b) The paradox of subject in relation to signifier – here the paradox is that the subject cannot be without signifier insofar as the signifier represents the subject. However, this act

of representation also erases the subject. A major instance can be found in the compulsive personality structure which resists being reduced to a definition – since a definition is nothing but words – while equally being unable to exist without such a definition, because it is what represents it. (c) The paradox of the subject in relation to the drive lies in the fact that the more she tries to satisfy the drive, the stronger it grows, as in the Talmudic saying: "A man has a small limb; if he starves it, it's sated; if he sates it, it is hungry", (Babylonian Talmud, Tractate Sukkah 52:2) which is to say: the more our sexual desires are satisfied, the bigger they grow. (d) The paradox of the ego – "Why is it that I suffer, while I am not lacking for anything?" – is that, though the ostensible reason for suffering is lack, often we have a sense of yearning when we don't realize that what troubles us is lacking lack itself – overabundance.

3   The paradox of freedom of choice versus fate – the more persons are aware of their limited freedom, more freedom in those domains in which they are at liberty to choose becomes available. Another way of putting this is the more aware persons are of being moved by unconscious forces (or in Freud's words, acknowledging not being the proprietor of their own home), the better positioned they are to identify with their unconscious and thus to perceive the presence of their free will in those things they did not ostensibly choose.

4   Paradoxes resulting from leaving the choosing subject out of the picture. In the paradox of the liar, for instance, we have the person who articulates the sentence and the person who is the subject of the sentence. Once this is understood, the noncontradiction becomes obvious. Here I will review the developmental aspects of the moment of emerging subjecthood in the child's life and the moment later when the subject is erased as desire is repressed together with the desiring agency.

5   Paradoxes resulting from limited or mistaken use of metaphors, especially metaphors inspired by physics. This covers Freud's theory of drives which was inspired by thermodynamic theory, through the joint uses of paradoxes in quantum theory and psychoanalysis, to superstring theory which solves the contradictions between the theories of general and particular relativity, on the one hand, and quantum theory, on the other, by adding dimensions.

6   Paradoxes that stem from missing a higher dimension. Shifts from point to line, from line to surface, and from surface to volume can be represented topologically. From this mathematical, abstract perspective, there is an additional, fourth dimension, namely of space – which goes beyond the three intuitive perspectives: (a) While a point does not occupy real space, it has a symbolic existence. Similarly, neither signifier nor symbol describes real phenomena: they create a symbolic reality. Many paradoxes emerge because of our treating symbolic phenomena as though they were real. (b) While the line describes linearity and hierarchy, it fails to capture

rhizomatic or circular phenomena. While the former describes the discourse of the authority or master, the passage to the two-dimensional surface describes an analytical and ethico-analytical discourse. This discourse does not accept the authoritarian Other. The unconscious is structured like a language, which unfolds associatively, weblike, rather than in a linear manner. Once the psychoanalyst no longer relates to his or her patient's speech as if it was a linear phenomenon, but setting aside its temporal vector, approaches it like a text that can be read from a variety of angles – this allows him or her to reveal additional meanings.

(c) The movement from a two-dimensional to a three-dimensional topology allows us to think of the subject outside the structures of the inside-outside dichotomy. We could also call this a passage from seeing the individual as an isolated ego, separate from her or his surroundings, to seeing him or her as a subject, a figure in a narrative. (d) The fourth dimension of space cannot be grasped intuitively; it is captured in topological formulations and graphs. An example of this is the four-dimensional topological structure called the *cross-cap*. These topological tools describe situations in which container and contained turn inside out and are containing and contained at the same time. This is a useful image for our understanding of anxiety, which involves an internal and external threat simultaneously. The threat is constituted by unconscious internal contents but at the same time by them in an external, alien form. In his *The Uncanny* (Freud, 2001 [1919], p. 219), Freud describes this as a turning of the inside out, whereby the deepest internal content is experienced as no less alien than an external threat. Similar inversions occur between the positions of lover and beloved; between identification with a conscious that contains the unconscious or the other way around, an unconscious that contains the conscious. Additional instances are inversions between concepts like the superego and id, subject and language, and reality and symptom.

7   The paradox of time – whose foremost representation is in the logic of *afterwardsness*, referring to a double causality in which hindsight turns the past into a cause. This paradox rests in the double function of causality: not only "due to" (linear line from past till future) but also "for the sake of" – with the future constituting the reason for the past. Thus, a linear vector connects between the experience of distress and the need or wish to express or complain about it. Along the vector of afterwardsness, distress is produced to express or complain about it. This makes sense when we think about a past distress which was silenced and which can find expression through the staging of current distresses. Afterwardsness is often at work in psychic life: (a) It can appear in prose writing or in the punchline of a joke: a surprising interpretation can change the meaning of something already said. (b) The subject emerges because of the very assumption that it exists. As the parents attribute intentionality to the child, they implant an intending identity

within her or him. When they interpret a contraction in the child's face as a smile, they convey to the child that he or she meant to be communicating, to smile intentionally. (c) At the early stages of psychoanalysis, the analyst listens because the analysand has turned to psychoanalysis in order to talk. Later, it is the analyst's listening that becomes the reason for the analysand's talking. The listening presence of the analyst as well as the emerging transference relations cause the unconscious to produce things like dreams. (d) It is the suffering of the symptom that eventually functions as evidence of the thing which caused that suffering; like the dreamer pinching herself. When I pinch myself and feel the pain, it means that I am not dreaming. (e) While Freudian reconstruction is often perceived as historical in nature, Lacanian reconstruction stresses the rewriting that goes into the patient's current perception. (f) The present too takes on a different meaning if it is experienced with reference to the future, especially with a view of a final reckoning: "Have you lived according to the desire that is in you?" The implication is that we decide in the present with a view to the question with which choice we will feel more reconciled in the end. (g) The aspect of the future is not only determined by the moment of death but in the symbolic dimension, which exceeds the limits of organic existence. (h) Sometimes the last word tarries, failing to give its afterward-meaning to the first word. The latter stays suspended, without clear meaning. When the psychoanalyst makes a cut by ending the meeting, she does this intentionally at a certain moment: before the patient can say more. This is how she puts an end to the infinite slip-sliding between meanings, forcing the patient to take a position. The déjà vu experience is a special instance of afterwardsness unfolding simultaneously.

8   The paradox of the act describes the situation when a person performs an action, and this radically changes her or him. At that moment, the person who performed the act vanishes and instead someone else, who was not there before, appears. In topological terms, this can be put as follows: a cut is made across a surface. Is the cut located on the pre–cut surface or on the post–cut surface? The uncut surface was replaced by the cut surface, much like the subject changes in the act, splitting on the temporal axis into the subject-before and the subject-after the act. The act requires the subject to disappear and reappear as someone she or he is still unfamiliar with. Many situations involving anxiety or change aversiveness are well-explained when we consider them in terms of this formulation.

9   There are also, finally, paradoxes that cannot be solved, or that are not meant to be solved and stay that way, unsolved. These constitute states of anxiety, perplexity, wonder and creativity. Not all of existence is amenable to symbolic logic, to what can be put into words or quantified. This is what in Lacan's teaching is called the Real, an interpretable kernel of the symptom.

References

Babylonian Talmud, Tractate Sukkah 52:2

Freud, S. (2001 [1895]). Studies in hysteria. In J. Strachey (Trans.), *The standard edition* (Vol. 2). London: Vintage.

Freud, S. (2001 [1912–13]). Totem and taboo. In J. Strachey (Trans.), *The standard edition* (Vol. 13). London: Vintage.

Freud, S. (2001 [1919]). The uncanny. In J. Strachey (Trans.), *The standard edition* (Vol. 17). London: Vintage.

Freud, S., & Einstein, A. (2001 [1933]). Why war. In J. Strachey (Trans.), *The standard edition* (Vol. 22, p. 197). London: Vintage.

Kumar, M. (2011). *Quantum – Einstein, Bohr and the great debate about the nature of reality.* New York: Norton.

Wittgenstein, L. (2009). *Philosophical investigations.* Chichester: Wiley-Blackwell.

Chapter 1

The paradox of existence

The paradox of existence occurs in the domain of ontology, the part of philosophy that addresses questions of being. An object is something that is or exists – How did it come into being? How do objects emerge? In the Lacanian discourse, objects are things that may or may not exist, and it is this very fact that enables us to treat them as such: existent. For Lacan, the object is an object of need first and foremost: it is defined by need, and this need in turn is defined by the absence or lack of the object.

It is on condition only of its not being self-evident, or in other words of its not necessarily being present, that the object becomes an object of need. I must be thirsty if the word water is to have meaning when I drink it. Water must be missing to be defined. The definition circumscribes lack, thirst in this case. Hence the definition "water" is based on thirst, on the absence of water. There arises, for the Innuits of the North Pole, the need not to crash through the treacherous thin ice. To cater to this need, they discern shades of white that convey the various thicknesses of ice. Someone had to fall through the thin ice and into the cold water for a word for that precise shade of white to be invented. It is the yearning for a certain type of gratification that gives birth to an object: thus, acquisitiveness antecedes and creates property.

What is property? We have certain feelings and a sense of possessiveness about it. If we do not have these feelings, nothing will turn it into our property. An object comes to supply for a need, and the need is grounded in the lack of an object. In this sense, we can say that the object exists in so far as it can be absent.

From this, it follows that the subject who experiences lack precedes the object: the object would not have come into being were it not for the subject whose needs defined it. This is not self-evident: positivism claims that objects exist in a world that exists a priori; the subject is the one who defines them. On this approach, we learn to recognize and name these preexisting objects as we develop. For Lacan, as said, the process is inverse: subjective experience comes before objects, and the object emerges in the infantile psyche depending on the infant's needs, drives and desires. The encounter with the organic world forces the human creature to experience needs like hunger and thirst and the frustration of not having them satisfied. The distress of experiencing need

DOI: 10.4324/9781003232285-02

is only resolved when the object that satisfies the need comes to have a shape and a name, for example the mother's breast in the case of thirst and hunger. In the infant's experience, it achieves definition by way of an object only from the moment it has served to satisfy a need.

So here we have the paradox of existence. Things exist; they are defined as objects, because of and thanks to their absence, which is indispensable for making the subject experience lack. This way of seeing things cancels the dichotomy between object permanence in the affective sense (e.g., in attachment theory) and object permanence in the cognitive sense (e.g., in Piagetian developmental theory). Any cognitive definition of the object as a separate entity follows from a need that gave rise to it qua distinct object, as an object of need, and next, also, as an object of drive, demand or desire. If the object lacks the psychic value of coming in response to a need, it cannot be identified cognitively.

Lacan shows how Aristotle's preoccupation with categorizing phenomena in the animal and vegetable world follows the logic of "absence as a condition of presence". According to Aristotle, mammals as a category are defined by one attribute, namely, the breast – or *mamma* (Lacan, 1961–1962, Session 9, p. 110), but what is a breast? To answer that question, we must be able to point out creatures that have no breast. Then, when we first encounter a creature that does have one, we will be in the position to state that "it does not have the no-breast". It is the creatures without breast who serve as the necessary background against which we can distinguish a breast and define it. Absence inaugurates presence, producing it in so far as it is a phenomenon achieving its contours against a background.

One of my earliest memories is of myself telling my parents that I am going to sleep. I closed my eyes and said: "I am asleep", after which I immediately opened them to announce: "I am awake". I don't remember how they responded. They may have laughed. They may just have ignored me. I fell asleep. On awaking the next morning, I remembered I had been preoccupied as I was falling asleep. Again, I announced that I had woken up, but this time I had woken up after my consciousness had closed down, together with my closing eyes. This is how I discovered what consciousness was: this thing that also wakes up in the morning when you wake up. It was only by experiencing its absence that I discovered consciousness. I tried to stay awake to catch hold of my consciousness at the moment of its disappearance (as I fell asleep). Every morning I woke up disappointed, each time consciousness had eluded me at the very moment when I wasn't there to take note. This was my first encounter with the impossibility of being conscious of losing consciousness. No notion of consciousness had presented itself to me up until the moment when I experienced retroactively how it disappeared as I fell asleep. But once I saw that consciousness could also not be, it emerged as something, something in the world. More precisely, it was my desire to grab hold of consciousness and fall asleep without losing my grip that gave rise, for me, with hindsight, to the concept of consciousness.

How does this paradox of presence through absence manifest itself clinically in various afflictions and forms of distress? Or how can the analyst first construe these experiences of suffering in terms of this paradox, then to help solve them by not accepting their premises? Here for instance is a paradox we see frequently in the clinic: "I want her when she's not there, and don't want her when she is". A man stops loving a woman once he and she start a relationship, once she returns his love. He wants to fall in love, but infatuation passes soon. Desire wears off, and together with it the object's value disappear to thin air. This represents a paradox if we assume that the man's object of desire is the woman. After all, we would expect him to be satisfied once he manages to gain her love. The question that will dissolve this paradox turns to the nature of the man's object. Maybe the object is not the woman but the man's sense of self-value? Once this is where we situate the object, the following picture emerges: the woman's desire defines him as an object of the kind "desirable man". Had the woman been his object, he would have gone on desiring her even in her presence. After all, obtaining her love is not the same as "having" her. In fact, since she is a subject, there is no way of "having" her and so desiring her can continue in her presence.

While I have until now discussed the absence of object and its creation from a generic perspective, Lacan singles out three mythic variations concerning the missing object and the subject creating it. These are the clinical formations constituting the core of the Lacanian diagnostic system: psychosis, perversion and neurosis (including hysteric and obsessive personality structures).

If the object as such is situated in the gap between word and thing, then the oedipal replacement of the mother by the father is a metaphor for the essentially undefined thing being substituted by the defined and distinct word. In Lacan's terminology, this is captured by the transition from the Real to the Symbolic.

In the case of the psychotic person, the object is never lost in the first place. Psychotic people may treat words as if they were things: they may raise an arm to protect themselves when someone hurls a curse at them. Here the word appeared without replacing the thing. The gaze which relentlessly assails the paranoid person is that kind of a persisting object. At the same time, this gaze also defines the psychotic person as an object stuck in the field of vision of that gaze. The psychotic person herself or himself is a kind of object that never became separate from the mother's body. Paranoia is fear of being swallowed because the subject never separated from his or her surroundings. We can identify the psychotic person's inability to be separate and to absent himself or herself in the phenomenon of erotomania, where it seems to the psychotic person that everybody is attracted to him or her, out to sexually exploit him or her. It seems to the psychotic person that she or he is constantly present in the other's mind.

Regarding the person with a perverse personality structure, the object is absent; as a result, it can be defined qua object, but with an inherent lack in stability. Here the object shifts between a phase of separateness and a phase when it reverts to merging with the background, as it were, when it becomes indistinct as a figure. The perverse subject, too, undergoes separation, but only during the one phase, after which, in the other, he or she becomes indistinct from the other – usually the mother figure. There is not enough frustration attending the necessary separation from the mother required for subject formation. In the case of fetishism, we may observe an attempt to constitute the object. We might think, here, of a semi-object, like for instance the high-heeled shoe. This semi-object is connected to the body in a way that constitutes it as not entirely separate. The perverse person's *jouissance* (pleasure-pain-excitement) of the object involves the object's alternating existence and nonexistence. The semi-object exists, on the one hand: in that sense, it is separate from the body as something the body lacks. On the other hand, it is inextricably bound up with the body. This concurrent relating and non-relating to the body can be observed in masochistic behavior when the subject positions himself as the rejected, cast-off object, thus leaving a vacant place that is open to definition. On the one hand, the situation is a mere performance. He is not truly being cast off: the ritual, for him, is finite and in the end, he belongs to the person who just now rejected and humiliated him. In the necrophiliac personality, this becomes even more obvious. The soul that left the body has not totally left it; some life is left in the dead corpse. Life is the object which in effect is no longer present in the dead corpse; in the necrophiliac act, this object is restored to it once again.

In contrast with the perverse and psychotic subjects, the neurotic person has already undergone separation. Here there are both lack and desire. For the neurotic person, words, which are objects formed from the absence of actuality, are valid. The hysteric strategy of desire is to define the object as absent through a sense of being ill-treated: "The object exists but it isn't mine because I was treated unjustly and unfairly". This allows for the preservation of a positivist principle which posits that the object exists without being absent; its absence is an avoidable accident, a cruel caprice of someone out to dupe us, a state of affairs that must be protested. But the crucial point here is that this positivist principle only obtains in fantasy.

The obsessive strategy is to create desire by aiming at an impossible or forbidden target. Here is the statement that underpins the status of this type of obsessive object: "If only we could turn back the wheel of time, or if the powers that be only allowed us, surely then the coveted object would be ours". Obsessive persons believe that prohibition or impossibility are the reasons for lack and frustration. They therefore wait patiently for the powers that be to die, after which they will be set free and live unconstrained. The specter of authority continues to haunt them.

An unsolvable paradox is, as said, at the root of subject-object relations as such. Since absolute ownership of the other cannot be achieved, full gratification remains unattainable. The object exists to the extent it stays unattainable: what keeps it in place is not-wholly-satisfied desire. This is what bestows a sense of satisfaction, albeit partial. It is as the negative image of the experience of frustration that the object exists. When the figure is isolated from its background by means of a cut, this is done by means of metaphorically circling the knife around the potential object twice over. The first circular movement, or framing, takes the shape of a vague sense of frustration, clinically described as a feeling of restlessness, confusion or even anxiety. This is the stage at which lack becomes manifest, though a definition of the nature of this lack is still missing. On the next encircling, there is a sense of need the shape of whose gratification is already known; a fantasy has already formed of the gratification the object is likely to produce.

One of the names that psychoanalysis has for an object which exists in its absence is the phallus. This originates in the transformation of the actual male sexual organ, the penis, into a symbol; in other words, it is replaced by a signifier. The phallus, in human history and individual development, serves to produce primitive binaries. One such binary signals the sexual difference between men and women by pointing at its presence in men or absence in women. Another binary of this kind signals the presence or absence of sexual desire by means of its two different states: erection or flaccidity. A third binary is the absence and presence of the object that gratifies desire, for all desire, including sexual desire whose symbol is erection, exists provided its gratification, or the gratifying object, is absent. This is how Lacan came to call the process of symbolization by the name of *phallization* (Lacan, 1973 [1964], p. 187). The price paid for the transition from things to words is the loss of gratification, since the things, as said, are objects of gratification. And because phallization of the penis turns the latter into a symbol – among other things, of masculinity – it is, from that moment onward, no longer the thing itself, or in any case, it is no longer only or simply that. The symbolic value of the thing comes at the expense of its value as need-fulfillment. This is obvious in each of the three previously mentioned binaries: thus, phallization is not merely a cognitive process of replacement of thing by symbol, but it regulates the libido. Need becomes eroticized and thus any need – whether it is of food, drink, or nicotine consumption – fails to reach complete satisfaction. This is because substituting thing by symbol introduces the dimension of the intrinsic impossibility of full satisfaction.

There is for Lacan one primary psychosexual stage without which the others (oral, anal, etc.) cannot emerge, and this is the phallic stage. (He disagrees with the approach that gives all these psychosexual stages equal status.) The phallic stage occurs when language enters a human's existence. From the moment "the signifier" in Lacanian terminology – appears in the person's life, he or she is no longer driven by need, and it is desire that takes its place. Unlike need, desire, as mentioned, is never satisfied. Words will never sate us in the way that real objects may do. Phallization connotes the transition from the full gratification of need to desire which, while not leading to satisfaction on the organic level, does sustain the subject. It is desire that takes the subject to a condition described by: "I yearn, therefore I exist". Freud's psychosexual stages can be considered variations of phallization, a string of losses and the replacement of the lost object by signifiers – starting from loss of the breast, through loss of the anal object, up to the discovery of sexual difference, which is the loss of the possibility to be both man and woman simultaneously.

How is all this reflected clinically? A main objective of analysis is to help raise consciousness regarding one's desires. While depression is characterized by the absence of desire, in the case of anxiety, desire is often either unclear or unconscious. It is the aim of the analyst's intervention to lead her patient through anxiety – evidence of a hidden wish – toward the definition of the patient's object. The notion of "wish" here is loosely applied to include desires and drives, both conscious and unconscious. The goal is twofold: to reduce or overcome anxiety by clarifying the object of the wish and to help realize the wish.

A married patient, for instance, stayed in touch with a former girlfriend. She has been sending him letters in which she includes romantic hints. All he does is send her back confirmation: he has received the message. When she announced she was planning to visit the country in which he lived, letting him know she would like to meet him, he told his wife. His wife was angry, claiming he had compromised their mutual trust. He didn't see it that way: this was an old girlfriend who may still have feelings for him, but he never reciprocated her suggestions, he hadn't met with her, and now that the question of meeting her came up, he first consulted his wife. In his individual treatment, he said he nevertheless did not feel entirely at ease about it all. When I asked what he felt (assuming that this somewhat puzzling awkwardness might disclose the nature of his desire), it transpired that he had a sexual fantasy in which he was taking a passive role. So, when he was receiving letters, passively, he had been satisfying a sexual drive in fantasy. He moreover told me about a fantasy in which he was being passed around, like an object, between women. So, on a first delineation of the object, cut from its background, frustration and anxiety emerged in the form of inexplicable unease. On a second circumscription, this unease was named a wish for passivity. Further cuts were conducted several more times until he realized the pleasure he received from taking a position of surrender.

Another illustration of phallization is anorexia. If the object is grounded in its absence, we may say that the anorexic subject, who does not eat, eats exactly nothing. Absence here produces the object "nothing". When we say "Take this food and put it into your body", we fail to observe where they are at: rather than being in a state of emptiness that needs filling, they are in a state of fullness that requires evacuation for them to experience themselves. The subject is trying to rid himself or herself of something. The object is right there with him or her, and it consists of nothing. Work with anorexic patients, therefore, involves helping them give up on something, some object, rather than getting them to take in something (for instance food). We will not be able to face this problem if we consider the object as something of a material nature – like food. In psychoanalysis, an object must be void of matter.

Petit a

The major object that Lacan invented – the object of psychoanalysis – is the "*objet petit a*" – or the "object (little) a" as it has sometimes been translated into English (Lacan, 1965–1966, Session 10, p. 169). This *objet petit a* represents the lost thing, leaving behind the lack which is at the roots of subjectivity. This object cannot be replaced with a signifier that can be claimed or attained, not even with the "nothing" which the anorexic person claims.

One myth that configures this object concerns the lost breast, which the infant initially perceives as a part of its own body that was lost, then feels the need to reattach itself to the mother's body of which it subsequently became part, that is, the other's body. But the *objet petit a* is more radically lost than this suggests: after all, it is nowhere to be found, nowhere in the world, neither in the subject, nor in the other. The logical operation from which it emerges is the double negation.

There are phenomena, in the intersection between subject and other, which are outside the domain of the subject:

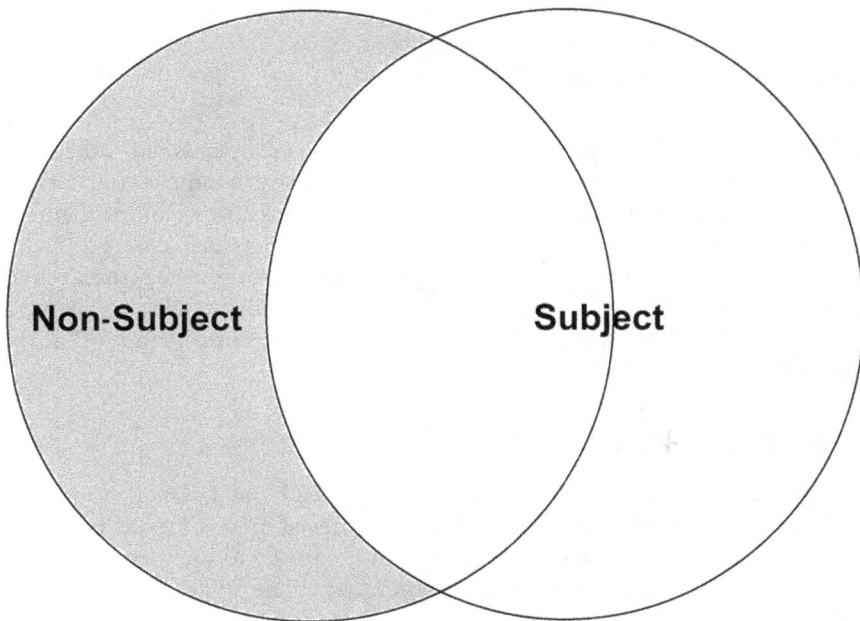

Figure 1.1 Outside the domain of the subject

Source: Original drawing by the author

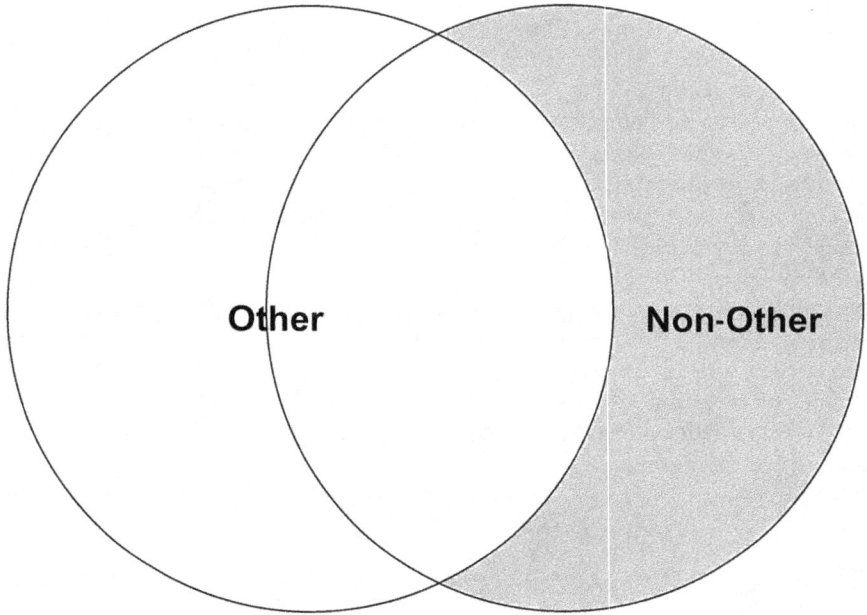

Figure 1.2 Outside the domain of the Other

Source: Original drawing by the author

From the Other's perspective, too, there exists an area that is not Other:

Double negation obtains for the intersection between subject and Other: what they share is what they both lack. It is a joint lack that connects them.

This domain of lack is a clearing in which objects can emerge. From the shared lack, intimacy arises. People can be brought together when they share their distress, the things they lack. This is why Lacan said about love: "To give what is absent to one who does not need it" (Lacan, 1965–1966).

Sexuality and love

One of the fundamental differences between Freud and Lacan is bound up with the question of genital sexuality. Freud never quite gave up believing that infantile polymorphous drives are bound eventually to integrate into adult sexuality. He hoped to resolve the common masculine splitting between the sexual figure of the polymorphous drives and the maternal figure of romantic love. Even though he never witnessed psychoanalysis succeeding to achieve this

**Non-
non-Subject
And
Non-
non-Other**

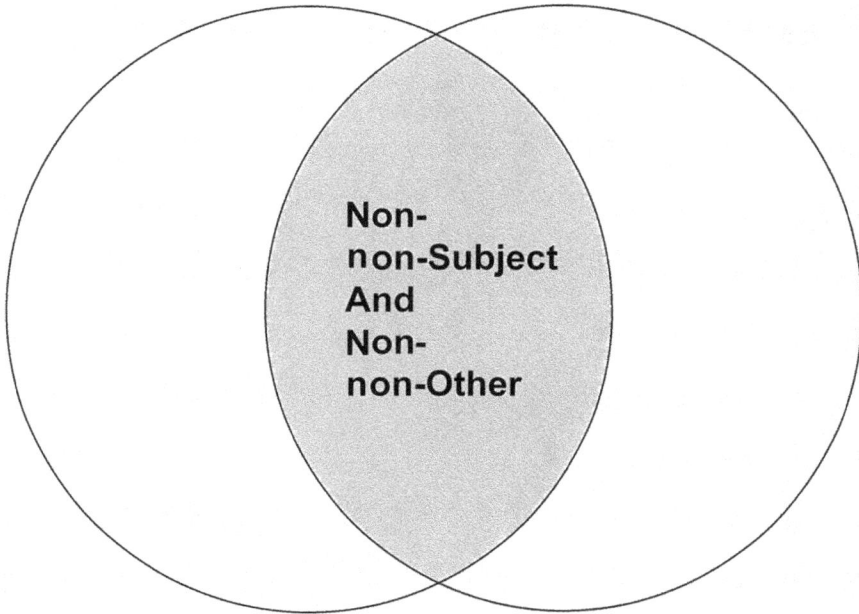

Figure 1.3 Non-Non-Subject and Non-Non-Other
Source: Original drawing by the author

for a patient, he felt this was due to the relative immaturity of the science he invented. In his "Analysis Terminable and Interminable" (Freud, 2001 [1937], p. 209), he expressed the hope that psychoanalysis would allow us to reach a genital stage, in other words, a sexuality that does not rely on dividing the body into separate parts (Lacan, 1960–1961, Session 16, p. 221). Freud's position reflected his *Zeitgeist*: clitoral orgasm was considered inferior to vaginal orgasm, which required penetration. It was a perspective that reflected a fantasy of sexual harmony.

For Lacan, analysis was always going to terminate on the side of the impossibility of genital harmony – both as a concrete phenomenon as well as a metaphor for the imperfect fit between word and thing. It reflected the fact that there is no full satisfaction, except for in depression (since desire depends on an unfillable absence, we may observe fullness in states of depression – even if it is a fullness of a kind that enables no yearning). Lacan considered any position based on the fantasy of genital perfection dangerous: in the name of perfection, the superego becomes strident and charged with aggression that is an expression of the id without limit.

References

Freud, S. (2001 [1937]). Analysis terminable and interminable. In J. Strachey (Trans.), *The standard edition* (Vol. 23, p. 209). London: Vintage.

Lacan, J. (1960–1961). *Seminar VIII – Transference* (C. Gallagher, Trans.). Unpublished manuscript.

Lacan, J. (1961–1962). *Seminar IX – Identification* (C. Gallagher, Trans.). Unpublished manuscript.

Lacan, J. (1965–1966). *Seminar XXIII – The object of psychoanalysis* (C. Gallagher, Trans.). Unpublished manuscript.

Lacan, J. (1973 [1964]). *The seminar of Jacques Lacan, Book XI: The four fundamental concepts of psychoanalysis* (A. Sheridan, Trans.). New York: Norton.

Chapter 2

The paradox of being

The subject exists under the condition of its lack, or "There's nothing more whole than a broken heart"

Subject without object

What goes for the object obtains, similarly, to the subject. The irreducible space between subject and object is the place from which the subject no less than the object emerges: the subject as holding a permanent lack. It is due to the subject's being imperfectly satisfied – and hence, due to its craving – that it emerges qua subject. Much like the object is constituted by virtue of its absence, the subject arises as a function of its desire. This is the other side of the absent object. Helen Keller offers us a singular description of the birth of the subject (Keller, 2010). Following an early infancy illness, Keller lost both sight and hearing. She grew up having nearly no communication with the outside world. Anne Sullivan, her teacher and companion for most of her life, tried to teach her sign language early on, using her fingertips to impress signs on Keller's hand. She put Keller's hand on her own lips and face when she was speaking. Moving her lips, Sullivan impressed the word "water" onto Helen Keller's hand while water, simultaneously, was running over Helen's hand. In doing so, she hoped that Keller would connect between the sensation of running water and the word "water". Keller didn't cooperate and grew unruly. She didn't get the point. The doll, with which she had been playing, fell on the ground and broke. Touching the fragments, she burst into tears. Sullivan, right then, guided Helen's hand back to the water, and again signed water onto her hand. Water was the first word through which Keller learned the link between things and words. In her memoirs, she describes how happy she was when the possibility of verbal communication with the world became available to her.

We might think of this event like this: the doll, once it broke, transformed retrospectively into an object. Until then, it seems, the doll served as a proto-object, whose objectivation was completed at the moment it shattered. In its unbroken state, in other words, the doll was not fully an object for the girl. Sullivan's effort to help Helen Keller connect between things and words depended on the loss of a thing, for as we know, a word replaces a thing. Just as I, when I was a boy, could relate to the existence of consciousness only once I noticed how it disappeared during sleep, Helen Keller could only think of the doll as something at

DOI: 10.4324/9781003232285-03

the moment the doll no longer was. The loss of the doll thus creates the lack that transformed Helen into a subject. Representation in memory is tantamount to the beginning of conceptualization or symbolization, which inaugurates the entry into language. In Lacanian terminology, this is the emergence of the signifier. Loss, object, subject and conceptualization in language all coincide in this scene – and they are wholly interlinked. Once a subject, Helen Keller could then use representations and exist, herself, in representation, as a subject of desire. Desire, as we know, depends on the experience of a gap between thing and word.

"Nothing's more whole than a broken heart" – this is because perfection is not available to us other than in our acceptance of loss. This is particularly obvious in the work with anxiety in children. Anxiety in children is often explained as a reaction to fear of abandonment. Afraid of losing the mother, the child clings to her. In the Lacanian approach, this causality applies in the reverse: what the child lacks is an experience of accepting loss; it is the knowledge that there is no solution to lack that will eventually assuage her anxiety. She must accept it and go on. In practice, this comes down to removing the child from the parental bedroom. The father must insist on sleeping with the mother again and not on the sofa, and the baby must move into its own room. Perhaps the child will be frustrated. Perhaps she will feel something is missing, but this lack will help her feel more present. The fear she might stop being will wear off. Fear, thus, represents a response to symbiosis with the mother where the child is erased in so far as she is an individual, a separate entity. Anxiety, fundamentally, is a response to incorporation, not to abandonment. It appears to be a response to abandonment because the child seeks to solve the problem by clinging. But we can think of this clinging as something that resembles what happens when someone is electrocuted: the hand muscles contract around the electrifying cable. Oedipal drives, too, draw the infant to cling to her mother, of course. But anxiety arises where there is a threat that these drives will materialize. Anxiety is the child's fear of her own drives. Obviously, it happens that children are abandoned and fear this may happen again, for instance in the case of adopted children. Mostly however, the anxious child is not post-traumatic in the wake of actual abandonment. A child cannot be expected to take her or his own distance from the mother. They cannot be expected to voluntarily submit themselves to lack. This is the parents' responsibility. Absence occurs anyway, always. Parents cannot always be there for their child. In that sense, parents don't ordinarily have to make any effort to make lack present to their child. What matters here is what message they convey. It is up to them not to convey to their child that there's something wrong when something or someone is lacking, for instance, by being apologetic. If the object is constituted from lack, because there is no object without words, the mother's absence can be made up for by some kind words, for instance, about the child being a big girl who managed to sleep alone. She will gain some satisfaction from such words.

The notion of existence refers to man as an organism. Being, by contrast, denotes man's state as a subject – given to language, and therefore to lack. The tension between existence and being is born out in the tension between sex and love. Existence involves a condition of immediate instinctual gratification, of a will to satisfaction. Premature ejaculation, in men, can be understood in terms of organic needs taking the upper hand. Where there is, by contrast, instinctual control, renunciation or delay of satisfaction, we observe a yielding of organic pleasure and the arrival of symbolic pleasure in its place. In return for immediate gratification, the man relishes the dignity of being a man who satisfies a woman. The subject is constituted on the side of being by means of a myth he adheres to – a myth about himself and the world, in which he features as a man who conquers his drives. This is how he realizes his masculinity. On the side of existence, at the same time, the pleasure of the body, the intoxication of the senses – there we can say that the subject is erased.

The act is another domain in which these tensions between existence and being are very palpable. An act is a life-changing action: getting married, getting divorced, starting or stopping studies, quitting a job, or losing one's virginity. It is an action which requires overcoming certain inhibitions. The act is so difficult because it involves becoming someone different. If getting married means changing from being single to being married – who carries out the act of the wedding? The single man transforms himself into a married man, and there is a moment during which he is neither the creator nor the thing created. To perform an act, a person must agree to not-be. The ultimate act, therefore, is suicide. But there is suicide in every act: the one who was the subject hitherto stops to be through the very deed he chose to do. And in doing so, he becomes someone he does not yet know. One patient kept failing to stop smoking until he formulated quitting as "stopping to be a smoker". Then he was able to perform the act and become someone else. What lay in the balance here was not simply giving up smoking but giving up on the smoker he had been to emerge, on the other side of the act, as someone else.

Acts typically differ in terms of the functions that change the subject as she or he disappears. In the case of the "passage to the act" (Lacan, 1966–1967, Session 12, pp. 70–79), a Lacanian term referring to an impulsive outburst, which even the subject herself or himself did not expect, the subject is replaced by the id. This is how a person can realize he's bleeding from his balled fist, the glass he's just shattered all around, without being conscious of it when he did it. Acting out, too, can be seen as an act: the unconscious takes over from the subject and speaks in actions rather than in words. The orgasm, in sex, erases the subject. The subject must be willing to not be in order to experience an orgasm. Often when a person is unable to climax, it is connected with her having difficulty in surrendering being for the sake of existence.

The subject relative to the signifier

The subject, over and beyond the object, also exists in relation to the signifier, to the drives, the ego and the other. Each of these modes of being is characterized by a different paradox. In the relations between subject and signifier, the paradox inheres in the satisfaction of desire. Here's a joke to illustrate this: What do you get when you cross an elephant with a rhino? Hell if I know. If the answer wasn't so ludicrous, it would have been frustrating, so completely does it fall short of satisfying our curiosity. We are (our curiosity is) not satisfied, and yet we are – that is the paradox. The relief of no longer having to go on chasing after meaning is satisfaction in its own right. How does it come to pass that we experience frustration as satisfaction? Freud had a neurological answer to this: a conversion occurs in the passage of time between when the neurological stimulus enters the system and the eventual occurrence of our motor reaction (Freud, 2001 [1887–1902], pp. 283–343). Freud suggested that the experience of suffering runs parallel to neural excitation, and that pleasure or calm is parallel to neural relaxation (he called this the pleasure principle). In the neural system, much like in an electronic system of cables and semi-conductors, some neurons reduce the stimulus they receive from other neurons, while others amplify it. Others, too, change the order, from excitation to inhibition, and vice versa. For example, when we exert ourselves with muscular effort, it can feel physically uncomfortable or even painful but at the same time on the psychological level, we may feel satisfied with our achievement. Freud sees this as the passage from a quantitative to a qualitative model (the amount of suffering is in terms of pace of neural activity vs the subject has influence over the experience of excitation; namely, whether it is experienced as suffering or satisfaction). And so, it can paradoxically happen that inhibition of (immediate) satisfaction is productive of satisfaction (in the shape of a future reward for restraint).

Systems that urge for immediate satisfaction are more ancient in terms of species and individual development. The satisfaction obtained by delayed gratification is determined by a higher instance, which determines whether satisfaction will become operative on taking food or on avoiding to do so. Such an inversion occurs conditional on having language: it is language that allows to replace immediate organic satisfaction with satisfaction derived from the adage "Who is the mighty one? He who conquers his drive" (*Babylonian Talmud. Pirkey Avot* 4:1) – a form of satisfaction that is all made of words. This is the inversion that language achieves when turning the organic pain of delayed gratification to meaningful pleasure. The possibilities of inversion made available by language as we turn to the object or reach for satisfaction are almost infinite. Eventually, this is how satisfaction moves from residing in the object as such to being achieved through language. This path never ends. Though there are types of forfeit of organic satisfaction that are pathological – for example, the consumption of nothing instead of nourishment in anorexia – there are other domains – for example, substance dependencies – where giving up on organic satisfaction for the sake of the pleasure of meaning is crucial to mental health. Any word we add may turn the tables: what we believed was desire (lack of and quest for satisfaction) turns out to be satisfaction.

One paradox of the relations between subject and signifier is that the latter is what makes the subject but also simultaneously replaces and subdues it. As the signifier can also constitute a most heavy burden, there are plenty of symptoms accompanying the effort to overcome it. One of Lacan's formulations of the relations subject-signifier is: "A signifier represents a subject to another signifier" (Lacan, 2002 [1964], p. 713). One thing this suggests is that people are identified through their roles and names in the communication with others – who in their turn are identified through their names and roles. This mode of discursive being has a way of erasing – to some extent – Real existence by way of body and organism and replacing it by a virtual Imaginary-Symbolic mode of existence.

This is manifest in the obsessive symptom of hesitation or doubt. A patient cannot decide between taking up studies in law or business. After much wavering, he goes for law. Now he isn't sure: Criminal or civic? And so on. He is not sure what he wants, but no matter what the choice eventually is, it will be replaced by the signifier. It is as though he chronically hesitates by which signifier he will be erased. The concrete outcome, however, is that he avoids identification with a signifier: if he studies law, he will be a lawyer rather than any other professional – and this is what scares him. This threat of the signifier, however, is only as great at the power with which he endows it from the outset. The more expectation he puts into this title of lawyer as something that will make his life meaningful, the more frightening this excessive meaning becomes. All these doubts are fantastical: for no matter what he chooses, he is fated to be under the regime of signifiers. Another obsessive patient told me that he was thinking that he was thinking that he was thinking – and this ad infinitum: he was stuck in the pseudo-philosophical question that informs all obsessive thinking. When asked what he might be thinking of if he didn't have these thoughts, he answered, surprisingly: "About being attracted to women who are not my wife". The signifier had served to erase the Real – sexuality.

To what extent can the subject be represented by this signifier? Only to some extent, obviously. This goes for the non-obsessive person as well, but the obsessive person rebels against the totality of the signifier while at the same time yearning for exactly that totality. He intensely wishes for the signifier to produce his entire being. Again and again, however, he realizes that being erases existence.

We can interpret this impasse by reference to the dialectic of truth (Lacan, 1985, p. 61). This is a move Lacan observed in Freud's work on the case of Dora. Dora complained to Freud that her father, wishing to spend time with Frau K, was pushing her into the arms of Herr K. We might assume that Dora worried about voicing this criticism of her father, who was Freud's friend. Yet Freud agreed with her that this was what her father was doing. Freud was unhesitant to validate what she felt and saw, but the truth is dialectic. "Why are you cooperating with this?" he confronted her with her choices. Freud's empathy when she expressed the pain her father caused her, allowed her to acknowledge her own part. Similarly, the obsessive person pretends innocence when it comes to empowering the signifier to the point of its overtaking. Borrowing from Dora's hysteric conversion, we may address the obsessive doubter as follows: "Granted, the signifier is overpowering, but what's your part when you attribute such importance to it?"

The signifier comes from the Other. We are born into language. By means of naming, our parents pass on to us their desires and those they absorbed from their forebears. The obsessive person highlights the signifier's coming from the Other, while the person with hysteria puts the weight on the encounter itself with the Other. The former lives with her thoughts, formed by signifiers, while the latter lives with the one who exchanges signifiers with her. As the subject is the product of signifiers and relations with people with whom she exchanges signifiers, the Other's desire is her desire. The compulsive person structures her desire like a demand coming at her from the Other. This issues in another paradox: "I refuse the thing that I asked to be demanded". Extracting desire from avoidance works in the following way: (a) I want (for instance, "I want to be a lawyer"); (b) I must be what I want ("Being a lawyer defines me"); (c) I am forced to do what I want ("Wherever there is a command, there is an Other, who makes the injunction"); (d) I refuse. This is how the wish transforms into an injunction that must be refused.

The tripartite encounter between language, the subject and the body produces a mechanism that generates objects. In the course of one cycle of desire and satisfaction, of the absence and presence of the satisfying thing, a representation of the absent thing evolves: it is the combination of this representation of the thing in its absence together with the thing present that constitutes the object. The word, which replaces the thing in itself as it is prior to verbal representation, is, by contrast, consistent. Unlike Heraclites's ever-changing stream, the verbal object is unchanging. This enables us to treat it as existent and to experience satisfaction. When the word first appears as substitute to an object, it disappoints: when we tell a child he's a "good boy" instead of giving him a sweet, he won't be satisfied. But next time he hears "good boy" he will register a sense of satisfaction. The second mention of the word has the effect of transforming the first mention into a lack that it, the second mention, fills. Hence the sense of satisfaction. In other words, the second time around the child already knew that being a good boy was something he wanted. We can observe a paradox in the fact that the thing that gave satisfaction was void. It is repetition, even if it is a repetition of nothing, that has an effect of satisfaction.

Bertrand Russell, the philosopher, drew the distinction between the things we count (heads, sheep or apples) and the numbers we use to count these things (Lacan, 1961–1962, p. 6). It is not the thing itself, he argued, that we count: it is not the thing itself that returns. There is only this one singular and specific

apple, with its wholly specific flecks in their wholly specific places, occupying its place and time. The signifier "apple", much like a sticker or label, gets
stuck to each thing in the crate of apples. What we count is that label: it is
what repeats itself. However, it is virtual and devoid of real matter. In terms
of mathematical group theory, this is the empty group. What all these apples
have in common is that in the act of counting, they all turn into empty groups.
When someone dehumanizes another person, humiliating him by treating him
like an object, he erases his singularity. This is what the obsessive person, by
fluctuating between possibilities, seeks to avoid. The same signifier, however,
also offers permanence and stability, recurrence – the satisfaction that the Symbolic order can give.

The person in love sighs with relief: "I was sure I couldn't fall in love again,
but look at me now, there's butterflies in my stomach!" He feels reassured –
calm – because of feeling excited (again). That's a paradox. Language is what
makes it possible to experience absence as presence, to turn hunger from being
an organic lack into a semantic presence – as in the phrase "I got my appetite
back" – the speaker can make hunger into satisfaction and then again into
desire, endlessly – and the same goes for the anorexic person who will not give
up the object "nothing".

Russell voided things of their content and distilled them into countable
labels. Descartes did the same for humans, reducing them to a function of
doubt: I doubt, therefore I am. To this, the obsessive person adds the following things: "As a person who doubts, I exist – else I am crushed by the fictive
truth of the signifier". To this, the psychoanalyst will comment: "To the extent
that you wish the signifier will completely represent you". Though the signifiers "nothing" or "doubt" are empty, this is not due to their meaning: they
are empty because all signifiers are empty, and all signifiers give satisfaction by
virtue of their iterability. In our symbolic life, we consume words and feel satisfied as a result. But in addition to being subjects, we also are living beings: we
feel real hunger and real satisfaction when we meet our organic need for food.

For the neurotic man whose father separated him from his mother by introducing him into the culture and giving him the possibility to delay gratification,
words are valid. Though the hysterical person might protest against the other
who introduces the signifier, and the obsessive person might protest against
the signifier as such – neither of them has the option to be free of these things.
If the obsessive person first hallows the absolute nature of the signifier, then to
try and break out of the prison he himself has built – in the case of the perverse
person, the signifier is not hallowed in principle. She, the perverse person,
scoffs at the sanctity of the signifier as the neurotic civilization around her sees
it. Masoch, who gave his name to the masochistic perversity, turned himself
into a dog, drawn along the stage by its collar by a dominatrix. Had he not
winked in the direction of the audience, we might have assumed he identified
with the signifier "dog". His gesture in the direction of the audience, however,
discloses that it was all put on, a performance. One story, however, the perverse

person cannot avoid: this is the story about a person who claims about a certain story that it's nothing but a story. The father, in the case of the perverse person, is located between being absent and being present; for instance, a father who carries a certain status in the community, while the child sees him humiliated by the mother at home. It is this position of the father that makes for the ambiguous, perverse position of his child, boy or girl, in relation to the signifier: the wink in the direction of the audience implying it's all a show, while also letting them know that the wink itself, too, is part of a ritual. Now, as opposed to the compulsive quarrel with the signifier or the perverse denial, the psychotic person's trouble is that he cannot believe in the signifier's value. Experiencing the signifier as an unlivable lie, he is subject to paranoia: it is as if he were surrounded by liars pretending that words are the actual things they denote.

As said, the passage from thing to signifier equates the passage from mother to father. Clinical structures situate a subject's various positions vis-à-vis the signifier at the oedipal stage. Never having separated from his mother, the psychotic person experiences her presence as an ongoing threat. The signifier, for him, has no validity. He lives in things. Treatment with a psychotic patient requires that the analyst serve as a symbolic scaffold supporting the former as a subject. Because the symbolic system for the psychotic person is unstable, he needs constant external support.

Subject in relation to drive: "Man has a small limb, if he satiates it its craving will increase, but if he starves it, its hunger will be satisfied" (Babylonian Talmud, Tractate Sukkah 72:2)

When we satisfy the urge, it grows: that's the crux of the paradox in the relations between subject and drive. It is a paradox arising from a mix-up between drive and need. While need is organic and hence sating it leads to release, the drive includes signifiers, and this subjects it to the laws of metonymy: meaning slips from one signifier to another. Such slippage testifies to the incorrigible wish for a perfect fit between thing and signifier. This failure to fit is responsible for the subject's fated lack of satisfaction, due to its dependence on the signifier. Lacan drew our attention to the fact that Strachey's English translation of Freud's works includes an error. We might call it his English Freudian slip. Translating the German *Trieb*, Strachey used the English word *instinct* rather than *drive*. While the instinct is in the body, the drive resides between body and signifier. Desire is always of a subject in language: it is the symbolic aspect of the drive, which constitutes the subject and gives meaning to her or his life. Thus, for instance, the role of a calling or vocation is not its realization but to enable a life with a calling. The drive, we may say, is situated somewhere between the need or instinct, and desire: its ties to both the body and the subject.

Here too, what Lacan calls the principle of phallization applies (Lacan, 1993 [1955], p. 55). Language leads to the erotization of instincts and biological needs like eating, defecating or genital tension and release. In the case of an eating disorder, the connection between eating and satisfaction comes to grief. This happens because of a transformation of need to drive, which in its turn makes it difficult to continue speaking in terms of hunger and satiation. When, instead of eating food, one eats the name of the food, or the knowledge that it is tasty, then there is no organic satiety. The drive then becomes chronically unsatiated. Even sexual tension and release must pass through phallization for there to be an erotic experience. In the absence of fantasy, of a story – unconscious though it may be – sex is felt as a merely physical experience, a release of pressure. One example of what happens where symbolic erotics vanish is disgust with sexuality.

Freud said, in "Project for a Scientific Psychology" (Freud, 2001 [1887–1902], pp. 283–343), that the primary instinctive impulse can follow a variety of paths. It can be blocked; it can be filtered and only receive partial response; its tension may be tolerated or it may be released instinctively without symbolic mediation; hallucinatory satisfaction may be obtained through the imagination, or the impulse may be transformed by means of a signifier, then to become subject to symbolic actions like repression, transformation and so on. Transformation to the symbolic system produces a desire that cannot be satisfied by fulfilling the need. No matter what it is, it is no longer the same thing.

Patients often seek treatment because they feel overwhelmed by their drives – this may involve a diet or some substance dependence, or else it may relate to anxiety or depression, which can be the outcome of the unidentified action of drives. The more convinced the patient is that it's a need, and therefore can be satisfied, the more unsatisfied she will be with her drive. Compulsivity is the outcome of an attempt to satisfy a need based on the mistaken assumption that the lack of satisfaction really originates in the need. "There is a small organ in man which satisfies him when in hunger and makes him hunger when satisfied, as it is said, when they were starved, they became full" (*Babylonian Talmud, Tractate Sukkah* 72:2). The more convinced one is that a yearning or desire, originating from a certain placement in a narrative, can be fulfilled as if it were an organic need, the more intense the drive's activity grows, exposing the Sisyphean side of the organic effort. A wealth of examples presents itself illustrating this mechanism. For instance, the harder you try to reconstruct a first love, the further removed you get from settling for a second love. As the original object is different from the present one, every effort to reconstruct it is bound to emphasize the gap. One objective of psychoanalytic treatment is for the patient to become cognizant of the infinite nature of the attempt to gain full satisfaction.

Each movement along the loops, 1D, 2D, 3D . . . that make up the torus symbolizes demand, the patient's frustration with the fact that the drive cannot be satisfied. If he passes through this process sufficient times, he will eventually agree to see the structural dissatisfaction.

The hole at the torus's center symbolizes the desire that is not meant to be fulfilled: this is what we experience when we exhaust all attempts at demanding satisfaction to the point that we understand is impossible to obtain it. The

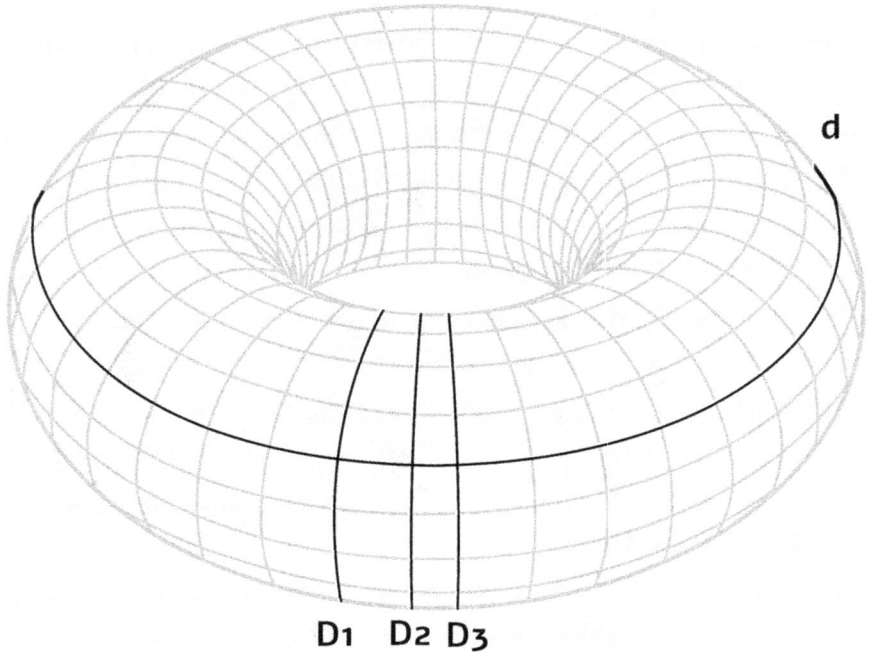

Figure 2.1 Demand D and Desire d

Source: Adapted image under creative commons license from https://commons.wikimedia.
org/wiki/File:Torus_cycles.svg by author https://commons.wikimedia.org/wiki/User:
Krishnavedala

excessive repetitiveness of D (Demand) circumscribes d (desire). The treatment aims to achieve a sufficient level of frustration in the matter of drive satisfaction (this we can consider a paradox, on the assumption that the treatment also aims to allow greater satisfaction).

One model describing the process of satisfaction is by reference to discharge, as if it is about offloading the contents of a warehouse. When we say something like "Just let him vent his anger. Let him get rid of it", we apply a model of need on the reality of a drive. This mistake only causes the anger to grow. Anger is not some organic matter that can be offloaded. It is the product of a language system which includes memories and meanings. If you get a machine to work, it will simply continue its action. A solution requires a different model: treating the patient's rage obliges us to stop the machine (rather than offload it). The patient must grow aware of the never-ending nature of the symptom and of the buttons that operate this machine. He will realize that these buttons and switches consist of words.

A similar logic is at work when children complain, as they often do, that they are afraid words will run out – as though there were a storehouse of words whose contents may come to an end. Freud might have added to this confusion when he used the metaphor of the steam engine to describe the drives. Lacan pointed out the connection between drive and language, and so the model he proposed was of a cybernetic algorithm, a machine. When we are unsure whether something a patient tells us is a delusion or recollected trauma, it may be critical whether we approach this by means of a storehouse model or a machine model. This is relevant not only to discharging (as opposed to arousing) the drives but also touches on situations when discharge is of unconscious contents into consciousness. Where we confront trauma, we might want to encourage discharge from the repository of unconscious memories to consciousness. But if we got it wrong, and what we have here is a delusion, our attention might encourage the delusional machine to rev up and work harder, to stimulate the patient to elaborate the delusion, while it would have subsided if we treated it with less interest.

We may think of free association as a way of getting the symbolic machine to work, warm up its engine (over and beyond the search for unconscious material, the main signifiers in the patient's biography). As desire is bound up with words, for as long as the machine works, there is desire. Depression is a state in which the machine does not work. One thing the length of the psychoanalytic session, which is not fixed in Lacanian psychoanalysis, allows for is to make a halt or caesura at a point when the symbolic system is in motion, which in turns allows the movement between the signifiers to continue after the meeting. Halting at the moment of insight can unravel a cascade of related insights. Stopping at the moment of remembrance can have an effect of recalling more and more.

Another aspect of the interrelations subject-drive is the extent of the subject's identification with her or his drive. Which of the two types does it resemble: "That's mine!" or "That's me!"? In the previously quoted paradox – "If he satiates it the craving will increase, but if he starves it, its hunger will be satisfied" – the drive takes the form of a "small limb", which is separate from the subject. In another approach, the subject and the small limb are not perceived as apart: "When I eat, I become hungrier, when I fast, I become more satisfied". Where subject and limb are experienced as separate testifies to the fact that language divides the body into parts and the body experiences infinite frustration due to the gap between subject and limb. The limb, where instinct, or the body is located, may be sated but the subject, which exists among signifiers, isn't. The self is not the limb, and the subject is not the organism.

The degree of alienation between subject and drive is likely to affect the subject's feeling of satisfaction. If the subject calls his drives "hormones", say, he keeps them at arm's length. To what extent can he experience satisfaction from a drive from which he is alienated? The power of an inversion like "satiating it will increase the craving" inheres in the way it underlines the repression that goes into the subject's stating "That drive is not mine!" Treatment aims for the subject to take responsibility for his drives, which among other things weakens their hold on him. If he says, "hormones", we might tell him: "Ah, you mean: you're attracted". It is about this that Freud wrote "Wo Es war, soll Ich werden" – where It was, there I should become (Lacan, 1957–1958, Session 27, p. 363). These words are an invitation to identify with the drives: to be more conscious of them to make their vitality more accessible to the subject – whether the latter eventually acts upon them or not. The subject, when it is linked to the drives in its modes of action, has a great deal of energy at its disposal. If moreover it is the organism's goal to satisfy need, then the subject's goal is not to satisfy the drive but to come into being by means of the drive.

The subject in relation to the ego: "If I don't lack anything, then why do I suffer?"

The following paradox often makes an appearance in the clinic: "I have everything I could possibly want, everything I wished for, so why am I still miserable?" Here too, the answer can be found in the question itself: there is a confusion between ego and subject and a misconception that the latter can be satisfied, and that satisfaction is the solution to unhappiness. Let's look at their respective development, ego and subject, to observe how they differ.

While the subject is based in lack, the ego fundamentally inheres in plenitude. The latter is the outcome of the young child's response to its physical inferiority to the adults and the tragic fact that it's cognitively able to be aware of this situation. This results in an illusion that the others are perfect and in a wish to be perfect like them. The child's reference point to such possible perfection is its own mirror image. This mirror image which he sees from the outside is the same one that everyone else sees. This mirror image is "the way others see me". This is the one the others refer to when they say "Sweet child". The two-dimensional mirror image lacks nothing and when the child identifies with its mirror image, it believes it can be perfect just like that image. And so, the ego takes it shape from the image of the whole body as it appears from the outside. Many of us are familiar with the experience of walking along in the street and suddenly discovering a stranger walking by our side. It takes a fraction of a moment until we realize that what we see is only ourselves reflected in a shop window. In this split second of recognition, we are gripped by a fear that our own appearance was so foreign to us. This is the moment when I see how I look when I don't imagine that the body image is me.

Modifying Sartre's statement to the effect that hell is the other (Lacan, 1988 [1953], p. 224), Lacan argues that the other becomes hell when he assumes the perfect mirror image and thereby instills a sense of inferiority. If in addition I manage to believe that this mirror image is me, then I'm even worse off. Now depression enters, for there is no lack where there is perfection, and where there is no lack, there is no desire. Desire is reserved for the subject who lives in language. The subject, like a word in a sentence, gains meaning from her or his context: when there is no story, no plot in which the subject lives, there is no goal either and no desire. This ego fosters an ideal of autonomy, a fantasy of nondependence, of glorious aloneness, of being self-made as if he, rather than his parents, had given birth to himself. This fantasy is based on a positivist perception of the individual as object, a hermetic thing, separate from its surroundings (as opposed to belonging in a narrative which requires mutual dependence with other subjects in the plot).

When a subject asks us, "How come I am whole and miserable nevertheless?" we will therefore reply: "You are unhappy because you identify with yourself as an ego, while your existence as a subject is contextual". The subject is a creature in a grid, a texture of semantic links to other signifiers and subjects. We may say that the subject is ecological: unless we render ourselves an account of its relations with its surroundings, we cannot talk about it. It is in language, among words, that the subject lives (as Helen Keller described so well).

A patient describes two states to which he is susceptible. He shifts between a sense of superiority in his professional status and an immediately following sense of inferiority, together with an addiction to sex. He forgets himself in sex, forgets he exists. This oblivion serves as a break from the painful feelings of inferiority of his ego, with its attendant fluctuations. He lives, we could say, in two registers. One is the imaginary register of the ego, which is dominated by competitiveness and inferiority; the other is the register of the real, marked by sensual intoxication and erasure. Here are his own words: "It's either being damaged, or to be sensually intoxicated". The following interpretation pointed at a third possibility of being a subject: "Or: to be". Since it is not possible to be, to feel experience, unless one is a subject with a lack – the alternative to having a lack is not to be at all. An ego that demands perfection allows for no being. Even Shakespeare's Hamlet agreed to be, to stop being his mother's object, only once he acknowledged the lack inscribed by the poisoned dagger. Only then did he choose to be an acting subject with his desire.

A patient once said to me, in tears: "I don't know who I am". In other words, I am not the full ego I am supposed to be and I don't know how to go about becoming one. I replied: "You are the one who is crying"; "You are the one who is yearning to yearn" (what we have here is desire, even if it is a hysterical desire that involves suffering). From a logical perspective, this interpretation seeks to solve a paradox by expanding the field of vision so it comes to include – over and beyond the ego's realm in which wholeness or perfection will lead to satisfaction, which then will bring happiness – an additional dimension, which is that of the subject. This is where the logical principle "I lack; hence I crave, and hence I exist" obtains.

References

Babylonian Talmud. Pirkey Avot 4:1.
Babylonian Talmud. Tractate Sukkah 72:2.

Freud, S. (2001 [1887–1902]). Project for a scientific psychology. In J. Strachey (Trans.), *The standard edition* (Vol. 1). London: Vintage.

Keller, H. (2010). *The story of my life*. New York: Penguin Putnam.

Lacan, J. (1957–1958). *Seminar V – The formation of the unconscious* (C. Gallagher, Trans.). Unpublished manuscript, Session 27, p. 363.

Lacan, J. (1961–1962). *Seminar IX – Identification* (C. Gallagher, Trans.). Unpublished manuscript.

Lacan, J. (1966–1967). *Seminar XIV – Logic of Phantasm* (C. Gallagher, Trans.). Unpublished manuscript.

Lacan, J. (1985). Intervention on transference. In J. Mitchell & J. Rose (Eds. & Trans.), *Feminine sexuality*. New York: Norton.

Lacan, J. (1988 [1953]). *The seminar of Jacques Lacan, seminar I – Freud's papers on technique* (J. Forrester, Trans.). New York: Norton.

Lacan, J. (1993 [1955]). *The seminar of Jacques Lacan, seminar III – The psychoses* (R. Grigg, Trans.). New York: Norton.

Lacan, J. (2002 [1964]). Position of the unconscious. In B. Fink (Trans.), *Ecrits*. New York: Norton.

Chapter 3

All is foreseen, and freedom of choice is granted

The paradox of fate versus free choice (*Babylonian Talmud, Pirkey Avot* 15:3)

Often people seek psychological treatment because they feel they aren't fully in charge of their fate. Once confronted with the analyst's interpretations, suggesting his unconscious choices and making him aware of the events and messages that shaped his life, the patient learns how he is indeed ruled by fate, especially that of the signifier. Certain words, spoken in his vicinity or ones he spoke himself, were inscribed in his psyche and prescribed some of his unconsciously made choices (which are hence hard simply to call choices). Now he understands he has been even less free than he imagined, but he sees, too, that he could be freer – exactly now that he is aware of the threats to and constraints on that freedom. Can we imagine someone who chooses unconsciously yet has the ability to choose how to dictate his future fate? Freud's response to the ancient saying "All is foreseen, and freedom of choice is granted" is that man is not to blame for a choice unconsciously made. And yet he is responsible for it. After all he is the one to have made the choice, even if unknowingly.

Classical tragedy has a paradoxical answer to the question of the relations between fate and personal responsibility: the more one identifies with a complete ego which is in competent control of its world – whether it is Oedipus in flight from his homeland, or the merchant's servant from Baghdad escaping Death all the way to Samarra – fate is bound to show that hubris will fail. By extension, we may say that the greater a patient's claim on controlling her choices, and the more powerfully she denies the role of the unconscious, the more persistently the symptom will make unconscious desire present. Where, by contrast, the hubris of consciousness takes a step back and curiosity about unconscious intention enters, the freedom of choice expands. Recognizing the fate determined by signifiers which, like cards she was dealt, were not the patient's choice, means a surrender of the fantasy of controlling fate. At the same time, she gains a certain freedom to play with these cards, that is, the signifiers that decide her drives and her fate. One objective of psychoanalytic treatment is for the patient to become aware of the existence of the unconscious. Free associations allow issues to come floating up and surprise the

DOI: 10.4324/9781003232285-04

patient. This sets a Copernican process into motion, one in which the patient gets to see herself as a satellite of someone else who is more herself than she thought, rather than as the center of her own existence. Listening to her own free associations, she observes the text that constitutes her psychic tissue. She observes to what extent she is the product of the narrative of her unconscious, the vocabulary stored in her unconscious which originates in the speaking environment, in other words, the Other.

We usually tie this abstract fate of the signifier or language to a tyrannical parental figure because it enables us to blame and complain: the matter seems not merely personal but also reversible. That's what Dora does when she complains to Freud about her father who, like a procurer, offers her to Herr K. Freud's response elucidates what he thinks about the question of fate and personal responsibility.

Once the patient realizes how active her unconscious is, this often ushers in her infatuation with analysis. The interpretive machine works overtime, trying to analyze each dream or slip of the tongue, each time as if a new continent was being discovered. But eventually – it may take a long time – the adventure of meaning is exhausted. A symptom initially seemed meaningless and then gained meaning through interpretation; or it was interpreted and then attenuated – yet there's a residue, something nevertheless remains. As consciousness opens itself to desire, there is less need for the symptom to speak the desire – and yet something remains, a stubborn core. This is not open to interpretation, and here the patient finds herself confronted again, helplessly, by fate. Words she heard as a child and determined her pleasure-pain-excitement, or what Lacan calls *jouissance*, have become part of her – no matter how deeply she managed to penetrate the myths, brimful of meaning, in which she initially wrapped herself. Traumatic triggers will upset the post-traumatic person even after she has healed from the trauma's semantic burden. "It" will go on speaking after she stops asking "What does it mean?"

At the completion of Lacanian psychoanalytic training, the analysand is reconciled with the fate of the signifier. This allows the psychoanalyst to accompany a patient on the road to creating meaning and losing it. While it is best for the patient to forget that free associations are nothing but words, the analyst must never do so. The patient must forget so that her words have the impact of deeds, because of which, words will lead to deeds. But while language is reality, it is not actuality. We must in the end know how to deal with lack of meaning, the illusion of free choice. Identification as a subject, in the sense of being a subject in language or object of the analytic discourse, allows the new psychoanalyst to conduct the treatment, rather than as an active agent, by trusting that free associations will do the job. The role of the psychoanalyst is to allow the ritual to take place, the associations to keep coming, much like in Freud's metaphor of interpretation as an act of clearing away broken twigs and any other detritus that get in the way of the free flow of associations (Fink, 2007, p. 80).

References

Babylonian Talmud, Pirkey Avot 15:3.

Fink, B. (2007). *Fundamentals of psychoanalytic technique.* New York: Norton.

Lacan, J. (1985). Intervention on transference. In J. Mitchell & J. Rose (Eds. & Trans.), *Feminine sexuality.* New York: Norton.

Chapter 4

Putting the subject into the picture

Lacan discussed a story Freud told about his little daughter Anna who on account of an upset stomach had to refrain from eating several foods she loved (Lacan, 1958–1959, Session 4, p. 41). At night, she spoke from her sleep, from a dream: "Anna Fweud, stwawbewwies, wild stwawbewwies, omblet, pudden!" (Freud, 2001 [1900], p. 130) – the things she had not been allowed to eat earlier that day. Anna, as a subject, is present by name in this passage. Freud's colleagues in the psychoanalytic association responded by saying that pigs dreamed of acorns and geese of corn: each dreams of what they love to eat. Lacan disagrees. While the goose might dream of corn, he doesn't dream about the goose who is himself, wanting corn. To allow for the statement "Anna Fweud . . .", what is needed is a subject present in her own existence as a desiring subject. Anna's dream was dreamt in a developmental register that precedes the function of censorship repressing so-called impolite desires and drives. When desires are repressed, the desiring subject is repressed along with them; this is how the subject exits the picture. At this stage, which is where Anna Freud in this vignette is situated, the child says: "I have three siblings: Paul, Ernst, and I" (Freud, 2001 [1900], p. 48). The one who does the counting, counts herself in as one of her own siblings and doesn't drop herself from the sentence. The mental possibility of stating "I have two brothers" requires from the one who counts to elide herself from the counting. In doing so, the third sibling, the one who does the counting, is not really erased: she is marked as erased, repressed. We can most emphatically identify her, in exactly that quality.

Unlike Anna, who is present in her statement, the next patient to whose dream Freud refers is old enough to have developed a neurotic tendency (both repression and the unconscious here are in place), leading him to drop himself from the statement qua subject (Freud, 2001 [1900], p. 42). The deceased father of the dreamer appears in the dream, addressing him as usual. The son is pained on behalf of the father who doesn't seem to know he is dead, and he is aggrieved at the possibility of telling his father this is the case, because then the father will have to know he is dead. In the dream, he feels it pains him to let the father know he is dead (Freud, 2001 [1900], p. 430). This dream came to him frequently in the months following his father's death. Since Freud assumed

DOI: 10.4324/9781003232285-05

that a wish appears in a dream as realized – that is, had the wish been for the father to come back to life and to feel good about this resurrection, the patient could have dreamed just that. For Freud, this dream does not feature the wish for the father to come back to life. What, then, causes the sorrow? That the father is dead? The possibility that the father knew he was dead? That would be the conscious, articulated part of the dream. But if we open the lens a bit wider and include the subject in the picture, then what seems conspicuously absent is the subject's wish for the father to be dead. The statement that includes this expression is the following: "It pains me to let him know that he is dead . . . as I wished". In his *L'étourdit*, Lacan puts this succinctly: "That one might be saying (*Qu'on dise*) remains forgotten behind what is said in what is heard" (Lacan, 1973, Scilicet 4: 5–52). Something, in other words, is being said behind the statement. Unlike Anna Freud, Freud's patient omits himself together with the fact that he is the one saying it. What is left is the statement alone.

Here is another illustration of how Freud restored the subject. Having told a patient of his that there is a wish behind every dream, the patient came back reporting on a dream in which she and her mother-in-law are together in a pension in the mountains: "How can you say there is wish fulfillment here? I cannot stand my mother in law", she challenged Freud. "Your wish is to prove my theory wrong", replied Freud.

In psychosis, God often takes the place of the subject. He serves as an abstract perspective that wills things into being and according to his views. In his *Portrait of an Artist as a Young Man*, James Joyce recounts how he wrote down his address in concentric circles: I live in this and that street, in a certain neighborhood, in Dublin, in Ireland, in Europe, on earth, in the solar system, in the universe. Running out of further circles, he experienced a dread of infinity. In urgent need of another, overarching address to complete the rest, he decided there must be some kind of a string that surrounds and defines everything else. This is the all-embracing gaze: the vacant place of the subject who has been removed from the picture, has been taken by the abstract gaze of God.

The divine perspective, absolute, and imagined as objective, is nothing but a way of dispossessing the subject, along with her or his subjective point of view. The concept of an abstract knower allows for a structured knowledge. Thus, the logical statement: "Knowledge exists within the knower" suggests a belief in a knower of the kind that enables a formulation of knowledge (attributed to the knower). In treatment, the objective is to achieve a release from the myth of the external agent, the Other, whose intentions and will shape the subject's fate. The patient must come to recognize the arbitrary, accidental nature, and the structural necessity and meaninglessness, of the unconscious signifiers that run her life.

In the case of little Anna Freud, the subject is present; in that of the dreamer about his dead father, the subject is repressed, and in Joyce's account, the subject is replaced by the Other. How, though, do we describe the world before the birth of the subject? In Freud's article "A Child is Being Beaten" (Freud,

2001 [1912–13]b), the one who is beaten appears in three variations: first as a child, next, as a narrator who considers himself a beaten child, and finally, as the brother of the child or as another beaten child. In Freud's eyes, what occurs is a gradual removal of repressions. The real issue is a sadistic need to see another child being beaten, but it takes time to acknowledge the repressed truth, which was there all along. According to Lacan, this can only obtain if we assume an already existing subject who is then being repressed. But can something like this happen even before the subject emerges? A beaten child can be the object of an aggressive drive even before the distinction between self and other emerges, in other words, prior to the appearance of an ego, language, syntactic rules that separate the passive and the active aspects of the drive. In the beginning, the child is neither me, you nor he, he is "it". Only when he is beaten does he become someone; a subject represented by a signifier. The self-reference to "It", for Freud, is the outcome of repressing the ego. For Lacan, however, "it" has a real existence prior to the emergence of the ego: the ego, rather than somehow being left out, has not yet come into existence. There are at this point no first, second and third person singular. As Lacan reads it, "A Child is Being Beaten" is not about the repression of the subject but denotes an event that precedes its formation. The blow itself is a signifier constituting a subject by virtue of delineating the limits of the body and subjecting it to the Other. Hence, on its first appearance, there is no subject, and the blow appears as a representation of the act of subject formation. This is reminiscent of what Helen Keller describes as the moment when the subject arises in the wake of the doll's breaking.

In the oedipal myth, it is the father who hits the child with the aim of limiting the omnipotence of its positioning as the object of the mother's desire. The blow releases the child from its place as the mother's object and enables it to become a subject. We can therefore say that what deals the blow is no other than the signifier, which splits the child between who she is as an organism and who she is for the Other, the agent of society and language. This act is of symbolic significance, there is not necessarily a memory of having experienced a blow. We might think of it as a fantasy, a myth, because such an event is so crucial for the founding of the subject that she manages to imagine it. Cutting or beating are key to any rite of passage (viz., circumcision, knighting). For Lacan, instances of the fantasy "a child is being beaten" first of all point to an as yet indistinct "it"; on a next appearance of the fantasy, it is the subject himself who is beaten, because the first appearance included the blow that transformed "it" into a subject. By the time the fantasy returns for a third time, the subject is already in place to validate the existence of the other, and hence, now, the other is beaten, signified, brought into existence. Freud too believed that the subject arises before the other: masochism antecedes sadism.

The analyst invites the analysand to take a point of view from which she can see that her wish created the symptom, dream and choices. She is invited to expand the lens so that she can see that she is part of the view, actively involved in the creation of her reality. One condition in which the lens is made wider to include the subject is obsessive compulsive disorder (OCD). In the case of the patient who dreamed of his dead father, the wish is repressed along with the one who wishes it, so that the subject is repressed. At the same time, we might observe a magical connection between wish and outcome. If the man suffering from OCD hates his father and at the same time loves him, he represses the hatred to reduce the tension of this ambivalence. The repressed hate transforms into a death wish and the magical belief that someone might die just because I hate him bestows actuality on this belief. Once the wish of the subject who wished it has been magically repressed, there remains only the reasonable possibility that his father will indeed die. Here the magical assumption features in a variety of rituals that come to protect the father. In *Totem and Taboo*, Freud explains that *magia* is a development of hallucination (Freud, 2001 [1912–13] a), in which things appear to happen by virtue of their very appearance in the imagination. Repression of the subject is repression of the magical connection between wish – a curse for instance – and realization of that wish. This is why a person with OCD will fear she might have killed a person without recollection of the violent feeling that would explain those thoughts as realizations of wishful fantasies.

How do we identify this subject in our clinical work? Sometimes, before recounting a dream, a patient may start by saying something like: "I dreamed this unrelated dream, but I'll tell you anyhow". He waits for a sign from the analyst that it's OK to start; he may apologize for the story the dream recounts; or else we may perceive a change in his tone. During these introductions, the dreaming subject is still present, introducing himself. His presence-as-speaker is repressed in the dream where he appears as the one who wants or dreams something. So, for instance, one patient says: "I'll tell you the story and keep it short", and then she proceeds with a dream in which a hairdresser cut her hair too short, and her subsequent annoyance. Bringing into account the subject from the introduction to the dream, we may interpret the existence of a desiring subject: "As you wanted, in short".

For the sake of repressing herself as a desiring subject, the patient separates between the statement in the dream and the act of enunciating the statement, as a way of taking ownership over the statement. It's as if she were saying: it's not me, it's just my dream. This is especially obvious where there is a dream within a dream: "I dreamed I was dreaming" (Freud, 2001 [1900], pp. 338, 575]), or "I dreamed I was waking up from a dream and then it turned out I woke up into another dream". Here the subject is twice removed from the dream; she is banished from the scene. The desire featuring in the dream belongs to the scriptwriter, not to the actor. While the actor appears in the dream, it is the scriptwriter who wished for this dream plot to exist. The actor's heart sinks when he thinks that he must tell his father that he (the father) is dead. It is the scriptwriter who killed the father. It is the latter whom we, psychotherapists and psychoanalysts, want to bring into the picture.

The refusal to bring the subject into the picture may be attended by anxiety. So, a person with stage fright might mistakenly assume his problem is a fear of criticism, but if we widen the lens to include the subject, the one who wants to be on the stage, we will understand his anxiety as Freud did: a refusal to acknowledge his own drives, in this case, an exhibitionistic drive. We will then attempt to find out why the exhibitionistic drive seems unacceptable to him. Was it forbidden in his childhood? Was he forbidden to compete with his narcissistic mother? We will make sense of the anxiety not as a fear of criticism as a performer but as a criticism of the very desire for the pleasure of taking the stage.

References

Freud, S. (2001 [1900]). The interpretation of dreams. In J. Strachey (Trans.), *The standard edition* (Vol. 4). London: Vintage.

Freud, S. (2001 [1912–13]a). Totem and taboo. In J. Strachey (Trans.), *The standard edition* (Vol. 13). London: Vintage.

Freud, S. (2001 [1912–13]b). A child is being beaten: A contribution to the study of the origin of sexual perversions. In J. Strachey (Trans.), *The standard edition* (Vol. 17). London: Vintage.

Lacan, J. (1958–1959). *Seminar VI – Desire and its interpretation* (C. Gallagher, Trans.). Unpublished manuscript.

Lacan, J. (1973). L'étourdit. *Scilicet, 4*, 5–52.

Chapter 5

Paradoxes resulting from choosing one physical paradigm which are solved by choosing another

From Freud's drives model to Lacan's cybernetic model

Some paradoxes arise from the limited nature of a specific metaphor we employ to explain phenomena. Metaphors from physics have been used before in psychoanalysis. I will discuss here the cul-de-sacs that some of them lead to, causing a certain theory to run into inner contradictions until the situation is solved by changing the physical paradigm. Paradigms deriving from the domain of physics are brought to be bear in psychological models each time a new concept in physics attains a degree of popularity. If, in the past, the world teemed with spirits and devils which could also make their way into the human soul, from the inception of the scientific era, physical and technological paradigms gradually came to describe the world and have also been adopted to talk about people. There were attempts, even before Freud, to conceptualize mental phenomena like hypnosis by reference to the prevalent physical model of electromagnetism, founded on the discovery of the commonalities between electricity and magnetism. This is the model underlying "animal magnetism", vital energy and Freud's libido. It is the *zeitgeist* that typically determines the physical paradigm. In Freud's case, one of the paradigms was thermodynamics, which emerged as an outcome of the industrial revolution. This was where the concept of the drive originated. The model assumes that where tension accumulates – like in an electric battery or a steam engine – it seeks release. Actual neurosis, Freud believed, was the result of such pressure – insufficient sexual release (Freud, 2001 [1898]). To this, he added another type of neurosis which he believed to originate from the refusal to know one's drives. As I have mentioned in the case of relations between subjects and their drives, the model of the storage space and its discharge doesn't work. In Lacan, the model is cybernetic-semantic: anger is ongoingly produced by an algorithm that operates continuously. The raw material here is not power, as with a steam engine, but knowledge. To make space for and give grounds to knowledge, Lacan is not tempted to take an animistic direction by assuming the existence of a knower. For him, the unconscious, being structured like a language, is knowledge that

DOI: 10.4324/9781003232285-06

works without a knower. There are, he believes reciprocities between words in the sense that meaning emerges when words are joined together in the conscious or unconscious mind, without the presence of an agent who brings them together. Here language acts spontaneously.

He wasn't an animist; already in 1954 (Lacan, 1988 [1954], p. 119), long before computers became as dominant as they have become, Lacan spoke about the "little machines [that] purr something new for us . . . one can't resolve the issue simply by saying that it is the builder who put it there". Lacan here is arguing that computers invent things that go beyond whatever contents they have been given by humans. They invent because they work analogically. They don't operate on a model whereby a person's input comes out as a product. Today we know that Google's translation engine generated a language (Wong, 2016), a type of new Esperanto which the computer can use to translate any language into any other language. This is an emergent phenomenon that appears out of nowhere. The engineers supplied the rules, but they didn't foresee the content that would be generated. Maybe we can say about the unconscious, as knowledge without a knower, that it is a type of artificial intelligence of language. This language implies a secondary plot in which there is choice and whose agent is the human individual. A successful analysis requires recognition of desire as something we must accept and live with even though we did not choose it.

To illustrate, someone experienced sexual abuse in his childhood, an event that stamped his later sexual life. This is the sexuality he has. Before he came to treatment, he was asexual, avoiding the zone of trauma. While treatment allows him to become sexual, it cannot be but within the terms of arousal that have been inscribed by the trauma. Do we say he chose, or do we say he didn't? He chose to stop resisting the thing that wasn't his choice. This is an incomplete answer to the paradox "All is foreseen and freedom of choice is granted" (*Babylonian Talmud, Tractate Sukkah* 3:15). To start with, the therapeutic process takes an opposite direction. Passivity is challenged; there is an invitation to take responsibility on the assumption that there is a function of choice. Toward the end of analysis, the patient is offered the opportunity to take responsibility for frustration. The movement is from thinking dominated by impotence and failure of narcissistic pretensions, toward acceptance of structural limitations and taking responsibility for impossibility. The latter means to accept fate as an a-personal algorithm made up of words and meanings.

Though Lacan does speak somewhat animistically about language – for instance, in discussing language as a parasite (Lacan, 1973, L'Etourdit, *Scilicet* 4: 5–52), he does so figuratively. Language determines desire without any intentionality; desire is generated by a-personal linguistic rules. In Seminar XI (Lacan, 1978 [1963–1964], p. 151), Lacan describes the transition from astrology to astronomy, from an animistic cosmology to a scientific one, as a process whereby the world was voided of the subjectivity with which it had been invested to be left without agency. Diverging from the animistic tendency, the human being can now conversely be likened to the world, and physicalist metaphors from now on can be applied to describe the human. Still, we must not forget that we are, here, in the realm of metaphors, and these can, and should, at times be shifted.

When Lacan conceptualized psychic causality as the outcome of structural laws, this is in parallel with cybernetic interrelations. This development is apparent, for example, in Newton's physics which affirmed that an apple will inevitably fall, and an arrow will continue on its trajectory because of the laws of physics rather than because of them having some sort of inner will to keep moving, as was the animistic belief that preceded it. Releasing the falling apple from animistic explications, Newton made room for the law of gravity. Taking context-dependent structurality even further, Einstein described gravity as an attribute of space. While it rolls down a two-dimensional slope, the apple's movement is produced by distortions in three-dimensional space. Similarly, the meaning of a word does not flow from some quality located inside the word itself – like the arrow's power to move autonomously – but is the result of its context: like the field of gravity in which the apple makes its fall.

From quantum mechanics to superstring theory

Heisenberg's uncertainty principle is a main component of the quantum paradigm. According to it, the act of measurement always affects its outcome. This means that there will always remain the quandary of our not knowing how the outcome might have looked without the interference of measurement. As concerns psychoanalysis, where the human subject is both the subject and the object of study, the influence of the researcher on her object of research is especially complicated. This is why Lacan answers the question whether psychoanalysis is a science in the same spirit as he approaches paradox – namely, by widening the lens:

> The question is: what does the psychoanalyst want, with this singular will which is that of desire? What is the desire of the analyst and we know for a long while that it is one and the same question as the following: what kind of science could include psychoanalysis in it?
>
> (Lacan, 1964–1965, p. 390)

In this science, the subject includes herself or himself in the research apparatus rather than being cut off it. The question of psychoanalysis's effectiveness cannot be asked separately from the analyst's desire to heal, even where that desire is not manifest other than through her or his willingness to be surprised by the revelation of the unconscious.

The subject is at the center of the difference between psychoanalysis and the other sciences. In the science that interests Lacan, the subject studies the subject without removing herself from the equation. What kind of science agrees to such a position? This type of science, Lacan answers, will not allow physicists like Robert Oppenheimer, whose work led to the invention of the nuclear bomb, to avoid the question of their desire in the light of the catastrophic implications of their research (Lacan, 1964–1965, p. 10). The removal of the scientist from this equation has scientific as well as moral implications. Lacan criticizes Kurt Goldstein who exposed dogs to random electroshocks to prove that anxiety is a response to helplessness (i.e., the inability to predict when the next shock will occur). Lacan interprets dogs' distress as a response to Goldstein's sadism. He criticizes him for leaving the subject out of his research and interprets this omission as a (scientific) Freudian error, of repressing his own sadism as a factor (Lacan, 1962–1963, Session 53).

Freud entered a place psychophysicists and others had not hitherto ventured into, namely, himself. In contrast with science, which considers the scientist's desire as a contamination of the scientific apparatus, psychoanalysis resembles alchemy, where the purity of the practitioner's soul is necessary to produce gold from lead (Lacan, 1978 [1963–1964], p. 9). The alchemical element in the psychoanalyst's psyche is her belief, resting on her professional experience, that the patient's symptoms and dreams carry meaning.

Quantum physics identified some paradoxes and rather blunt violations of natural laws as they had been formulated by earlier physicists and understood by human intuition. Such violations also appear in Lacanian psychoanalysis, which is cautious about intuitions and conceptual shortcuts, or heuristics. These paradoxes show up when we look at quantum phenomena from a limited Newtonian perspective. Following are the violations of quantum theory (Ben Dov, 1997).

With regard to the visual: While in Newtonian reality a particle is a well-defined object, quantum theory also includes phenomena that lack form. In quantum reality particle state blends into wave state and vice versa depending on the measuring equipment. We can ascribe quite a bit of human suffering to the side effects of giving shape to something that has none. Symptoms of hysterical conversion are an effort of the unconscious to situate formless conflict in or on the body. The attempt to solve the problem at this site only worsens the subject's condition (who is coping with conflict). Phobia can also be considered a response to anxiety triggered by something shapeless, or perhaps by shapelessness itself. Giving the formless thing the shape of a spider or some other phobic object may resolve the anxiety (while producing a phobia of a specific object in its place).

With regard to causality: In both Newtonian and Einstein's mechanics, processes are characterized by having a cause and an effect. One billiard ball hits another causing it to roll into the pocket. But in quantum theory there is no clear mechanics that can predict causality: what we have is probabilities. In the Lacanian model the relations between cause and effect may change direction: A symptom is a way of inventing a cause by assuming its existence in the light of an effect. This is nothing but a fabricated effect which comes to produce an ostensibly specific cause, which is in turn nothing but the uncertain, formless fact that we are trying to ground. The released prisoner, for instance, has as a symptom that he nearly misses the bus to work in the morning. This is in spite of work being very important to him, because it isn't at all easy for an ex-prisoner to find work. He explains how having run after the bus and narrowly catching it, he sits down with a sigh of relief, and thinking: "Phew! That's just in time!" His symptom supports the thought: "That's just in time!" which serves as an effect that presumes its own cause and thereby maintains it as such: "Through the nine years I spent in jail time stood still," and so, as a result, "I'm just in time". Thus, the symptom is like a smoke machine, enabling us to believe that there is a fire.

With regard to locality: Locality assumes that things occur at a specific site in space. The phenomenon of entanglement in quantum mechanics violates this assumption. A particle reacts to a manipulation of the twin-particle with which it is entangled, irrespective of the distance between them, and simultaneously. This is how language works for the subject: Having no location, language makes it impossible to unambiguously answer the question whether the subject speaks the language or is spoken by it. If we stick to the three dimensions of space, then one possible location of language is physiological, namely in the brain's temporal lobe, with neural extensions to other areas in the brain. Language, in this case, is situated within the subject. Another possibility is that language is located in culture, in the profusion of signifiers the subject receives, so that language surrounds the subject. So, is language located inside or outside the subject? Children or psychotic patients, who believe that their thoughts are transparent, grasp something about language. The words from which thought is made up don't have an inner life, as if they were locked into our skulls: they exist between subjects, in other words, they have a public aspect.

Locality came under question early on in psychoanalysis when Freud discovered repression: in the *Uncanny* (Freud, 2001 [1919]), he explains that the German word *unheimlich* is paradoxical because its meaning is identical to its opposite *heimlich*: both refer to what is ominous. While the *unheimlich* – or the uncanny – arouses terror because it is strange and unknown, the *heimlich* has the same effect because it involves the most repressed inner drives about which we wish to know nothing: this is the inner stranger. Lacan coined this the "extime" – something that is so intimate it is strange (Lacan, 1992 [1959], p. 139).

One wonders how many dimensions it takes for the paradoxes to disintegrate, paradoxes that emerge because of a lack of fit between Einsteinian physics, the behavior of the astronomical bodies and the quantum mechanics of subatomic particles. The physical theory of superstrings (Zwiebach, 2009) was developed by mathematicians and physicists who concluded that the clash between quantum physics and Einsteinian astrophysics is settled in an

11-dimensional universe. Following the tracks of Lacan who deployed topology and four-dimensional bodies more specifically, I suggest supra-dimensional thinking can be used in the clinic. With each added dimension, new conceptualizations of psychic phenomena become available.

References

Babylonian Talmud, Tractate Sukkah 3:15.

Ben Dov, Y. (1997). *Quantum theory: Reality and mystery*. Tel Aviv: Dvir (In Hebrew).

Freud, S. (2001 [1898]). Sexuality in the etiology of the neuroses. In J. Strachey (Trans.), *The standard edition* (Vol. 3). London: Vintage.

Freud, S. (2001 [1919]). The uncanny. In *The standard edition* (Vol. 17). London: Vintage.

Lacan, J. (1962–1963). *Seminar X – Anxiety* (C. Gallagher, Trans.). Unpublished manuscript, Session 53.

Lacan, J. (1964–1965). *Seminar XII: Crucial problems for psychoanalysis, four fundamental concepts of psychoanalysis*. New York: Norton, p. 151.

Lacan, J. (1973). L'Etourdit. *Scilicet, 4*, 5–52 (C. Gallagher, Trans.). Unpublished manuscript, p. 390.

Lacan, J. (1978 [1963–1964]). *The seminar of Jacques Lacan, Book XI: The four fundamental concepts of psychoanalysis*. New York: Norton.

Lacan, J. (1988 [1954]). *The seminar of Jacques Lacan, Book II: The ego in Freud's theory and in the technique of psychoanalysis* (S. Tonacelli, Trans.). New York: Norton.

Lacan, J. (1992 [1959]). *The seminar of Jacques Lacan, Book VII: The ethics of psychoanalysis* (D. Porter, Trans.). New York: Norton, p. 139.

Wong, Z. (2016). Google Translate AI invents its own language to translate with. Retrieved from www.newscientist.com/article/2114748-google-translate-ai-invents-its-own-language-to-translate-with/

Zwiebach, B. (2009). *A first course in string theory*. Cambridge, MA: Cambridge University Press.

Chapter 6

Dimensions

The dimensions of space

If we think in terms of dimensions, we can further open our lens so it can take in more of the scene without the two-dimensional constraints imposed by the visual metaphor. There are shifts from dimension zero, to dimension one, to two, three, and even to four dimensions. We can observe all these transitions in various basic clinical processes.

The point

The point constitutes the zero dimension: it is place without volume or area. The point represents the pure signifier, signifier without signified, without essence – like a number before we attach it to an apple to count the number of apples. When teaching simple math to young children, we use beads which are counted just like we count fingers. The "unary trait" – a term Lacan used, referring to Freud's earlier "single trait", is such a bead but one that is immaterial. It is the signifier, as mentioned, that creates signifieds as being identical. So, for instance, the signifier "furniture" may include table and chair, present them as equivalent and hence countable in the series of furniture. The word "furniture" does not refer to a particular type of furniture. It is attached to various phenomena so that they can be included under the signifier "furniture". If we had chosen to use the signifiers "table" and "chair", we could no longer count them under a common signifier. This principle can help us understand certain phenomena of coincidence. It is with the choice of a common signifier for different phenomena that coincidence emerges: "He phoned me exactly at the moment I was going to call him". It is up to me to define "a moment" – is it a minute or five minutes? – I might even have felt *at any given moment* that I was about to phone him.

Like the point, the pure signifier is a hole. It has no volume, no existence in the world. The signifier makes a hole in the Real (Lacan, 1958–1059, p. 235).

Before the signifier appeared, there was only physical matter in the world. Suddenly, another type of matter made its entry, signifier-matter; it came in the shape of the first signifier, the unary trait. It leaves a hole where there was only

DOI: 10.4324/9781003232285-07

matter. The signifier has generated antimatter in the sense of having introduced "no volume" into the world.

The Borromean knot, to which Lacan referred in his later teaching, renders the interdependence of the three registers of human existence: the Real, the Symbolic and the Imaginary. If one of them comes undone, so do the rest.

The actual strands that make up the knot forge a tie in which what holds the rings together is neither a common axis around which they are tied, nor a chain link, as in the case of interconnected rings. The point of connection of these strands rather than being local is the product of the relations among the three rings, the outcome of their being interwoven. When one pulls the rings into different directions, their point of connection transforms into a point in space, their point of friction.

Borromean modes of thinking allowed Lacan to rethink his clinical work. From an ontological perspective, this type of thinking clarifies that reality does

Figure 6.1 A loose Borromean knot
Source: Photograph by the author

Figure 6.2 A tight Borromean knot
Source: Photograph by the author

not equal some prior axis around which the human psyche organizes itself in its three registers (the Real, the Symbolic, and the Imaginary). Reality, rather, is the product of how these three registers interweave. So, we can think of psychosis as a condition in which the mythical central point around which reality can be organized is lacking; neurosis, by the same logic, can be understood as a condition when the rings are strongly pulled sideways and reality becomes overly clear and rigid. How would therapeutic work look that tightens the psychotic reality around a mythical center and, by contrast, loosens the neurotic reality?

Some neuro-cognitive models of neural networks (Hohwy, 2013) view the brain as a deductive machine geared to predict the nature of the object on the basis of incomplete data. Prediction is based on ongoing correlation between the internal statistical model, grounded in experience, on the one hand, and the external input; in this way, the result then allows for appropriate response to the input. Where the statistical model is confirmed, it is strengthened; where it is refuted, it weakens. As the model is more firmly corroborated, and one puts greater faith in the proven statistics, the risk of wrong prediction of external input increases. Where there is a gap between model and reality, unrelated energy is left over in the psyche – something we can see as analogous to what Freud called free energy. Such a gap may be experienced as surprise. A state of nirvana, in which the pleasure principle is fully operative, is a hypothetical state of perfect predictive ability, in which all libido is attached to something. It is also a state of full fetishization, where libidinal value is attached to all objects. The libido is the question, and the fetish is the answer. The aim of psychoanalysis in the case of psychosis is to tie free energy to semantic structures that subserve the subject, in other words, to help that subject to belong to a more coherent world. For the neurotic patient, reality is too coherent, and therefore treatment here looks to enable the libido to stray from its rigid anchoring, to loosen fixations. Lacanian technique makes it possible to cut a meeting in mid-sentence, when tension has peaked, to leave the patient in a state in which the free energy does not rapidly connect itself to a representation. In this way, the patient learns something about the relationship between signified and signifier not being obvious. Anxiety of course may be so intolerable that it is better to end with some statement that achieves a clear meaning. The idea is that the suspension of meaning, a stop on attributing sensory input to existing models, though possibly anxiety-arousing, may also stimulate desire.

The recognition, in the course of psychoanalysis, that there is no prior reality other than what the subject takes upon her or himself, allows, in addition to the simple acknowledgment of the existence of myth as such, consent to live according to it and participate in its composition. Psychotic patients do not have recourse to the pseudo-external anchoring the neurotic patients can use (the point in the Borromean knot) and nor do they have any other anchor. One conceptual solution of analysis in this case, is the addition of a fourth ring; it is interwoven with the existing three and will tighten the connections, producing an anchor that enables joint work on the registers, which in turn support in holding reality. Lacan calls this the *sinthome* (Lacan, 1975–1976, Session I, p. 1). One way in which the psychotic person creates the *sinthome* is through delusion; through an ideology with which she identifies, or another solution that enables her to feel of value to her surroundings.

Line

A line runs between points, and lines are distinguished in terms of the topology of relations among the points. Topological bodies differ from each other in how linear or authoritative they are.

Line or ring-shaped networks are the most linear as all the points they include have the same constrained motion on one axis only. In a tree-form network, the point at the top of the hierarchy has two-dimensional freedom: this point represents the Other, the authority, the center. This hierarchical

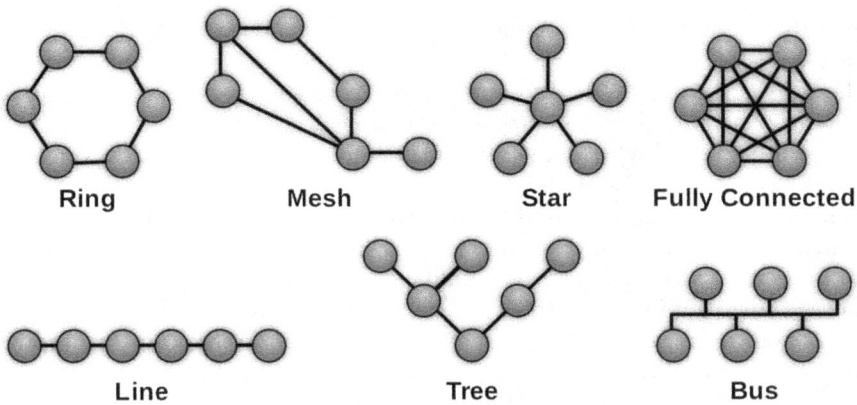

Figure 6.3 Types of topological networks

Source: Image under creative commons license from https://commons.wikimedia.org/wiki/ File:NetworkTopologies.png by author

structure branches off like a family genogram. The points at the head of the organization have more freedom of movement than those at the bottom of the hierarchy. The latter are limited to one axis of movement, and the topology for them remains linear. The bus, fully connected, star and mesh networks are all two-dimensional, and each point on them has freedom of movement on more than one axis. The fully connected network is the most rhizomatic of them all: here each point is related to each other point.

The decentralized rhizomatic network (Deleuze & Guattari, 1983) is an alternative to the authoritarian, hierarchical network. In psychoanalysis, rhizomatic thinking aims for the abolishment of absolute truths or of authoritarian moral judgments made in the name of normativity. When treatment starts, the patient hopes it will one day help him attain the ideal that the imaginary authorities of his life, often the parents, held out as a goal. Treatment, however, does not reach the ideal; it aims to change thinking itself to adopt a nonhierarchical structure and to remove the need to embody the ideal. Psychoanalysis aims to escape the grip of the linear and authoritarian, of thinking in terms of must, should no choice, right or wrong. When the analyst encounters his own prejudice and it gets in the way of taking a therapeutic stance, then he must return to analysis himself and free himself of it.

Getting rid of the Other on the condition of using him

One paradox that arises in the transition from linear one-dimensionality to rhizomatic two-dimensionality is that one has to get rid of the Other on the condition of using him, as Lacan put it (Laurent & Miller, 1989). Does the Other exist or doesn't he? Well, he doesn't, but he does exist as something we must be rid of. In "The Subversion of the Subject and the Dialectic of Desire in the Freudian Unconscious" (Lacan, 2002 [1964], p. 713), Lacan discusses the devil's question "What do you want?" in Jacques Cazotte's *The Devil in Love* (1772). This question raises the protagonist's anxiety. He does not know his own desire and when someone inquires after his wishes, it makes him feel that he doesn't know what they are. If he was faced with a specific demand, his anxiety of the unknown would subside. He cannot be sure he knows what the Other wants or that the other knows what he wants. The other's own access to his desire is very limited, since, unlike in the case of a demand, desire does not let itself be fully formulated. Still, the subject has his ideas about what the other's desire may be. Such ideas are a type of invention that comes to soothe the tension of mystery.

Right from the outset, the subject has no existence in a desire of its own without relation to an other: after all, the subject only emerges as a desiring subject when it enters language, and language always comes from the other, who remains the one in whom desire originates. It is the assumption of the other's desire, his intention to somehow take pleasure from the subject, and that the subject must protect himself against this – all of this is how the subject's desire begins to take shape.

The more the subject tends to perceive her desire as a demand coming to her from the other which gives the desire shape, the more likely she will be to refuse her own desire eventually. This is why getting rid of the Other on condition we use him should be understood as knowing that when I see him as taking a demanding attitude, this is a way of constituting my own wishes. In other words, claiming ownership of wishes that have been deposited with the other is one way of getting rid of the Other. We are bound to feel obligated to authority of all kinds (parents, the state, spouses, a fitness trainer), but an inversion allowing for the subject to accept her own desire becomes possible because of the recognition that relations with the Other are exchange relations (not only power relations). That's when it's no longer the authoritative Other but the counterpart as other. We can see this at work in the ways in which authority changes during a child's education. When parents convey to their child that there are things he must do, they keep in mind that it's a trick: nobody really must do anything. But parents like to teach their child that there is such a thing as an obligation in the first stages of life, just so he won't do dangerous or harmful things. Should they lose sight of the fact that it's a mere conceit, the parents may come to put obligation or duty above all else and lose themselves in a desperate struggle for its sake. Which will then make it plain for all to see that they are not even in control of themselves.

As the child grows up and starts challenging his parents about the nature of duty and obligation, the parents will admit to the sleight of hand in some cases, setting the child free to choose for herself. Now the parent, who still wishes to direct the child, is left with the ploy of the "price" as in the ethics of free choice, where every choice comes with its own price; this takes the place of a legal ethics with its imaginary obligations and punishments. With the arrival of adolescence and the adolescent's rebellion against parental authority, the parent should understand that what the adolescent wants is not just freedom of choice but also its opposite, namely, that the parent should force her to fulfill her duties.

Rebelliousness is paradoxically a last-ditch attempt to cling to the safety provided by authority, to remain exempted from free choice: "As long as I rebel, that means there's someone who is in charge of me". It is the parents' task to slowly wean the child from her faith in authority and pass her the message: "It's your life. You must do what you think right. But you should know that whatever you choose, it comes at a price". Probably the most difficult thing for the parent is to acknowledge her or his inability to decide for the child – and to put responsibility for her life with the child, even if it's hard for the latter to accept this.

Plane

The transition from the one-dimensional line to the planar two dimensions can, among other things, serve to describe the shift from speech to writing. There is a point to listening to the patient's words as if we were reading a written text. This is listening like "mind reading". When we read, it is easier to go back to things that were mentioned earlier, to listen without undue commitment to the linear order of things and consider them from several directions and perspectives. We might, for example, want to interpret an earlier dream with reference to a current one.

Another possibility opened by the move from line to plane is that it enables to think of simple parental authority – a united parental front facing the child – in terms of the transition to the complexity arising when the child shifts his libido from the mother to the father in the late stage of the oedipal development. At this point, things become more complicated: the mother loves the child, the child loves the father, and the father loves the mother. The triangular, oedipal scheme is projected on a planar surface (a triangle cannot be drawn on a one-dimensional line). The mother's role here is to understand the complexity and the two-dimensional character of the situation to come to terms with the ingratitude of her position: having dedicated herself so fully to the child, the child now turns its back on her and directs its love to the father. This happens as part of a three-partite deal in which she gets the father's love, the father gets the child's love, and the child gets the mother's love.

We may also describe the transition from ego to subject in terms of the move from line to plane. The ego is dominated by power relations on the axis of the ego facing the imaginary other, of master-slave relations, of a life-and-death duel between the subject who has a lack and its ideal mirror image. This is the one-dimensional axis of envy and rivalry, of inferiority and idealization, of identification and the zero-sum-game in which when the one rises, the other of necessity falls. The subject, by contrast, is located on a two-dimensional plane, allowing him to move from any specific point into any direction rather than being limited to one, up or down, motion (in other words, more or less in relation to the ideal).

It so happened that a man who had been my commander during my compulsory military service came to me for psychotherapy. At that time, he had been about eight ranks above me. Though I recognized him, he didn't, obviously, remember me. I didn't say anything. When he sought my professional help, our authority relations turned over. It took me some time to set aside my perception that I could not be a source of authority for someone who had been my commander. As far as my inherently hierarchical ego was concerned, the position of this superior was that of the imaginary Other. If one is to deploy the possibility of there being different situations (in one of these he is my superior, in another I take the position of the authority vis-à-vis him), one must have the capacity to perceive reality as planar, rather than being structured as a vertical line consisting of points.

Usually, at the start of treatment, the patient is situated on the one-dimensional axis of authority. What he expects to hear from the analyst comes, as far as he is concerned, from an authority. When he says: "It was hard to come in here today and tell you I went to the casino yet again . . .", this reveals to us that he sees the analyst in the role of the imaginary Other, in charge of self-control. The analyst's response does not have to chime in with the position into which she was cast. Eventually, this response should allow the patient to see that having positioned himself as the one who is to be blamed, he has also removed himself from the responsibility for his choice. A simple direct response like "Don't go to the casino" would confirm that the patient's strings are held by the analyst. Instead, one should address the patient as a subject, as one who lacks something. In this example of the casino, the patient treats the analyst as though the latter had been disturbed and disappointed. The analyst, in turn, returns the lack to the patient: "It seems that you are lacking someone who would set you limits".

Lacan uses a graph (Lacan, 2002) to illustrate the shift from dialogue between ego figures, and dialogue between a subject and her Other.

On the side of the ego, the communication the patient tries to have is on the one-dimensional axis, from point a, on the side of the psychoanalyst, to point a' on the side of the analysand. It is the psychoanalyst's goal to identify another axis of relations, between the psychoanalyst in the position of the Other (A) and the analysand in the subject position (S).

When a child returns from playschool, he shows the drawing he made to his parents, and they respond: "Great! You're a great painter!" – they encourage him to identify (as an ego) with the figure they seem to be addressing. Expressions of admiration are vital to a child's development, but if communication tilts too much in the direction of this axis, then when the child grows up, he might have a hard time knowing what he loves and prefers. A parent

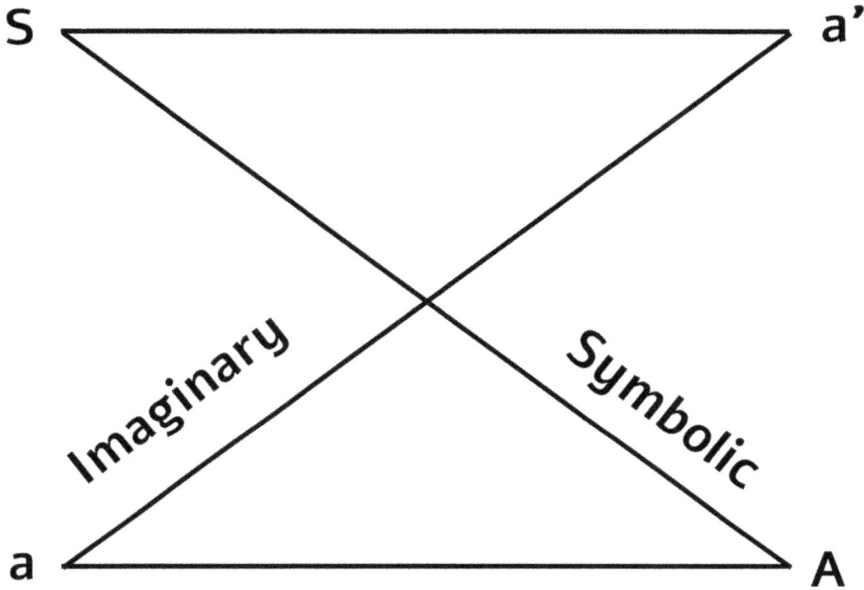

Figure 6.4 Schema L. by Jacques Lacan
Source: Reproduction by the author

might alternatively respond by commenting how much the child seems to love drawing. This puts the parent in the position not only of being a source of recognition for the child's ego but simultaneously pointing out, and thereby stimulating, the subject's desire. Similarly, when a person wants to discuss her professional future, then a question that is bound to elicit her desire would be: "What would you choose to do if in everything you did you would be average?" This way of asking neutralizes the ego's ambitiousness and competitiveness. Some people will feel uncomfortable with this question because all they want is to excel; they have no desire that doesn't pass through the ego.

In psychoanalysis, the ego axis is the axis of resistance. Here the patient is preoccupied with the communication with the analyst: his own thoughts about the analyst, and vice versa, what the analyst might think about him. This preoccupation will get in the way of psychoanalytic work with free association, of talk that isn't mainly for the sake of communication but rather comes to reveal the unconscious.

The paradox of resistance is that the analyst cannot at one and the same time occupy a position that rejects the imaginary Other while also taking exactly that position to interpret the resistance to surrendering *jouissance* (as opposed to defense against knowing the drive). Thus, where there is resistance, we must allow for conditions that allow it to disappear. The psychoanalyst must show the patient that he (the patient) resists authority only after having put it into place himself – and encourage him to examine why this is so. Since the patient will experience the interpretation "You imagine authority" as a statement of authority, the analyst will have to wait until the patient himself sees that authority is imaginary, and then to agree with him. Over and beyond this, the pleasure derived from the fantasy of authority must be identified to let go of this pleasure. Usually, this pleasure concerns being released from responsibility by appeal to the authority.

Volume – body

Some paradoxes hinge on seeing the subject structured in two-dimensional space, but if we would consider it in three-dimensional terms, the paradox would vanish.

The first and foremost effect of two-dimensional thinking is that it produces a clear distinction between inside and outside. This understanding then leads to the question whether, to discover one's real desires, one should retreat and turn inward, or rather move outward (consult other people, act in the world). Another question is whether we can say that sometimes a person is in a mood in which she turns inward, while in other moods she is directed outward. The inside-outside distinction is crucial to the process of individual development, and it is based on anchoring the identity within the closed contour of the mirror image. When it derails, this developmental process can lead to psychosis as in hallucinations (when thoughts sound like voices coming from outside). But in the work with neurotic structures, a change from this model to another

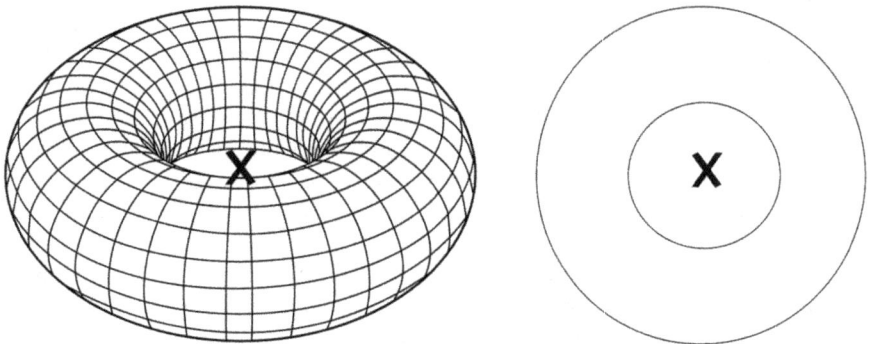

Figure 6.5 The center is outside the three-dimensional form and inside the two-dimensional form

Source: Adapted image under creative commons license from https://commons.wikimedia. org/wiki/File:Torus_cycles.svg by author https://commons.wikimedia.org/wiki/User: Krishnavedala

three-dimensional paradigm can be effective. This affords situations in which a movement inward achieves a movement out (which would be paradoxical in two-dimensional thinking). One way of looking at this is that the more exposed to himself a person is, the less he represses and the more authentic, the more connected he is to the world outside: less inhibited and more expressive.

Some critics claim that psychoanalysis removes a person from the real world and social involvement, causing him to take responsibility for no one but himself. Psychoanalysis is seen as offering its services only to some privileged people in their ivory towers, people who seek the narcissistic satisfaction of having an audience. In his *Psychoanalysis and Social Involvement* (Hadar, 2013), Uri Hadar refutes this argument by suggesting that Lacanian psychoanalysis allows the human individual to take a subject position that is more aware of, and hence more accountable for his wishes, a position in which he desires more. Since human existence as a subject implies the way the person is essentially embedded in language and society, analysis helps him to acknowledge that he is a contextual creature, like a word that takes on meaning in relation to its context. Psychoanalysis and social-ethical development are, therefore, one and the same thing. While the objective of analysis – to allow the subject to act – is to serve his mental health in the first place, we cannot separate this development from his social-ethical growth. Ethics, hence, is psychic health, and vice versa: being connected to oneself of necessity involves connection to the outside world. The division between inside and outside, the contrast between a distinct individual identity and the environment all derive from a notion of ego-based identity. This aspect of identification is obviously part of life, but the focus of analytic healing is the subject.

A Lacanian ethics aims at taking responsibility for the choice between desire and *jouissance*. The superego, constituting the Other as a tyrant, enables shirking responsibility for being a subject. When Adolf Eichmann argued that he had only done what he was told to do, he was not inventing pretexts: he was telling a truth. He took pleasure in positioning himself as a mere tool who has no responsibility for choices. Hadar explains how psychoanalysis sets the patient free of injunctions based on a belief in the Other, by placing the subject in the dimension of speech: he must take an ethical position without relying on information and facts supplied by the one in authority. The subject must take his position despite the lack in himself, as well as in the Other. The subject must act without having all the information at hand because information will always be lacking. This can only be achieved by taking one's place within the symbolic social order.

The fourth dimension of space

We cannot visualize a leap from the third to a fourth dimension. Since our concrete, palpable world has three spatial dimensions, a fourth dimension must be an abstract thought only. If the transition to three-dimensional space made it possible to eliminate the distinction between inside and outside, then the type of paradox we may be able to solve when thinking with four dimensions will be entailed by inversions like between big and small, part and whole, container and contained, and between object and subject.

Descartes pointed out a congruence between spatial axes in geometry, on the one hand, and algebraic equations with two or three variables, on the other.

If we take the equation X=Y=Z for instance, which describes volume, each time we advance one stage on one of the axes, we do the same on the two others. What about the equation X=Y=Z=W, an equation we can write down but cannot draw? Even though this cannot be achieved on the visual Cartesian axes (where the third axis [Z], drawn on a three-dimensional plane to suggest three-dimensionality), it is possible to calculate algebraic formulas including four dimensions and more. We can think of this in analogy to the shift it took to move from two to three dimensions. If we place a weight on a two-dimensional rubber sheet, this will make a dent, so that the situation is now three-dimensional. If next we throw a marble onto the sheet, it will circle

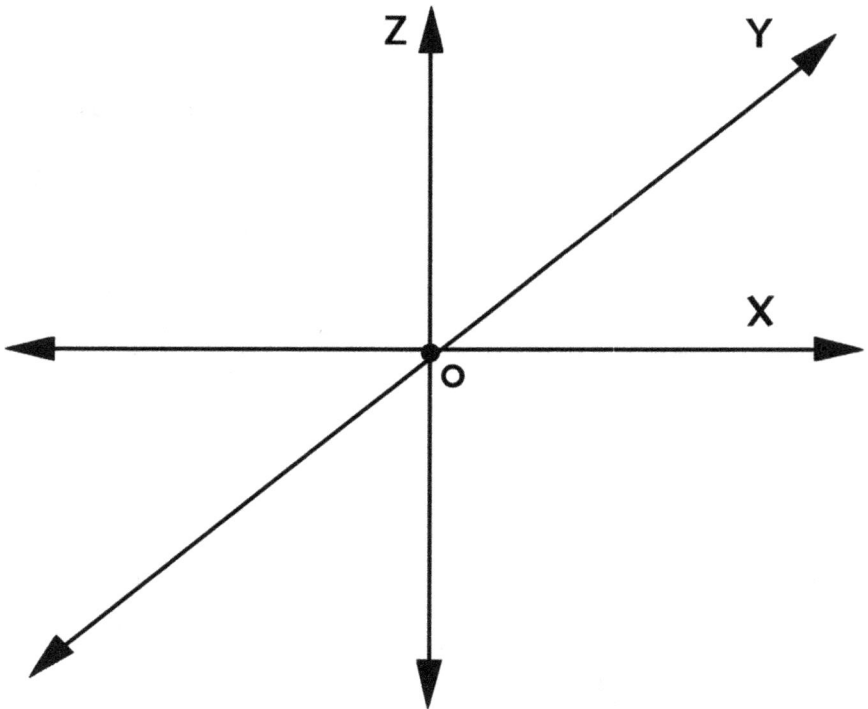

Figure 6.6 The Cartesian axes, X Y Z

Source: Original diagram by the author

around the depression and eventually reach its bottom. The dent, in three-dimensional space, is a metaphor for the hollow created by a heavy body in four-dimensional space. Light arriving from a very remote star, when it passes an exceptionally heavy astronomical body, will be diverted from its original track and drawn in the latter's direction. We could simply say that the gravitational force of this astronomical body attracts the light. At a more complex level of explanation, assuming a four-dimensional plane, the weight of the heavy object creates a scoop in three-dimensional space, distorting it and deflecting the light to its center, like in the case of the marble mentioned earlier. There are a number of topological objects whose existence though impossible in a three-dimensional world is possible in a four-dimensional one. Lacan uses these objects to illustrate phenomena like the conversion between container and contained. One such object is the cross-cap.

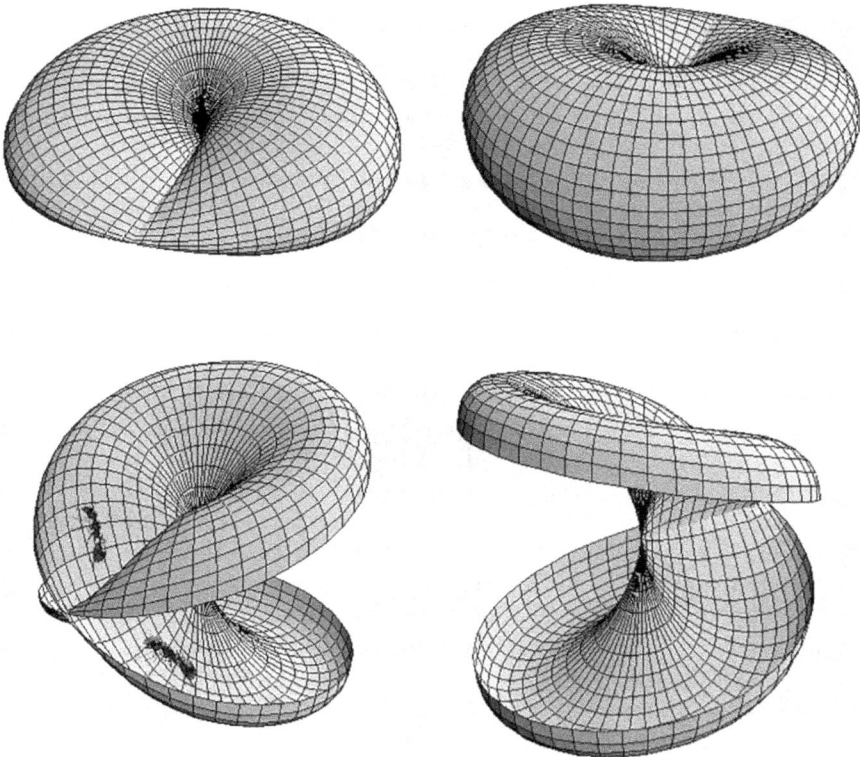

Figure 6.7 The topological cross-cap

Source: Adapted image under creative commons license from https://en.wikipedia.org/wiki/File:CrossCapTwoViews.PNG and https://en.wikipedia.org/wiki/File:CrossCap SlicedOpen.PNG by author

The cross-cap is a torus which bisects itself along one line in such a way that the floor on one side (where the ant can be seen on the right on Figure 6.7) turns into ceiling on the other side of the bisecting line (where the ant is on the left). What we see, in fact, is the same ant moving through the crossing-over ceiling, which folds over on the right-hand side, thereby obstructing the ant; the ant then finds itself on the roof of the twisted cylinder on the other side of the bisecting line, as though the obstructing ceiling does not get in the ant's way. It might be said that the ant moves through walls. Like in a science fiction film, the ant passes through super-space in the fourth dimension. In four-dimensional space, the floor plane on the right intersects with the ceiling plane on the left without mutually interfering – as if the other plane did not exist. The ant moves from the inside of the cylinder, in which it is contained, to the outside of the cylinder, the containing side.

Lacan refers to Edgar Allan Poe's story "The Purloined Letter" (Lacan, 2002, p. 3). The police prefect cannot find the letter even though he has his detectives cover every square centimeter of the apartment. Dupin the private detective succeeds where he fails: it was a letter left in plain sight but like an envelope turned inside out. This conversion between container and contained is missed by the prefect who only looked in three-dimensional space. Rudy Rucker, in *The Fourth Dimension: A Guided Tour of the Higher Universe* (Rucker, 1984), drawing an analogy with our ignorance of the fourth dimension, tells how the two-dimensional creature from Flatland panics when a three-dimensional finger enters his two-dimensional flat, which looks like a drawing. It is his shock at what he perceives as impossible that induces the panic. If he could make a dimensional leap, the impossibility of the finger inserting itself from nowhere would stand revealed as a movement in three-dimensional space. Sometimes, we can resolve a symptom or attenuate anxiety by opening the lens or jumping a dimension. At other times, we are stuck in our limitations. If it's not possible to conceptualize the conversion container/contained in the super-dimension, then we have no choice but to live with the anxiety.

This is also true of the phenomenon of the uncanny (Freud, 2001 [1919], pp. 237–240). As mentioned before, Freud explains that though the uncanny is what is strange and unknown to us, our own unconscious – internal and not external – is also uncanny to us. In his book *The House of Dolls*, the Israeli author Ka-tzetnik, who was a Holocaust survivor, describes his encounter with his own uncanny. Nightmares which plagued him ever since the Holocaust caused him to suffer from insomnia. He describes how, in LSD-induced hallucinations, part of a treatment he underwent in Switzerland, he had seen himself wearing a Nazi uniform. This recognition of the violent drives he himself harbored undid, we might say, the three-dimensional membrane between inside and outside. This is how he began sleeping quietly in the fourth dimension.

Object/subject conversion

Not a few paradoxes arise because of the mistaken assumption that in relation to some specific phenomenon, what's at issue is the object, while in fact it is the subject – and the other way around. This is borne out usefully by the geometric golden ratio (Lacan, 1966–1967). This golden ratio can be observed in the exact proportions of a rectangle such that if we divide it into two parts, and we turn one of the halves by 90 degrees, the same proportions are obtained. The ratio between length and width of an A4 sheet is identical to that of an A3 sheet, which is the size of two A4 sheets.

The ratio between a and b on the A4 sheet is identical to that between b and 2a on the A3 sheet. These proportions also return in the natural

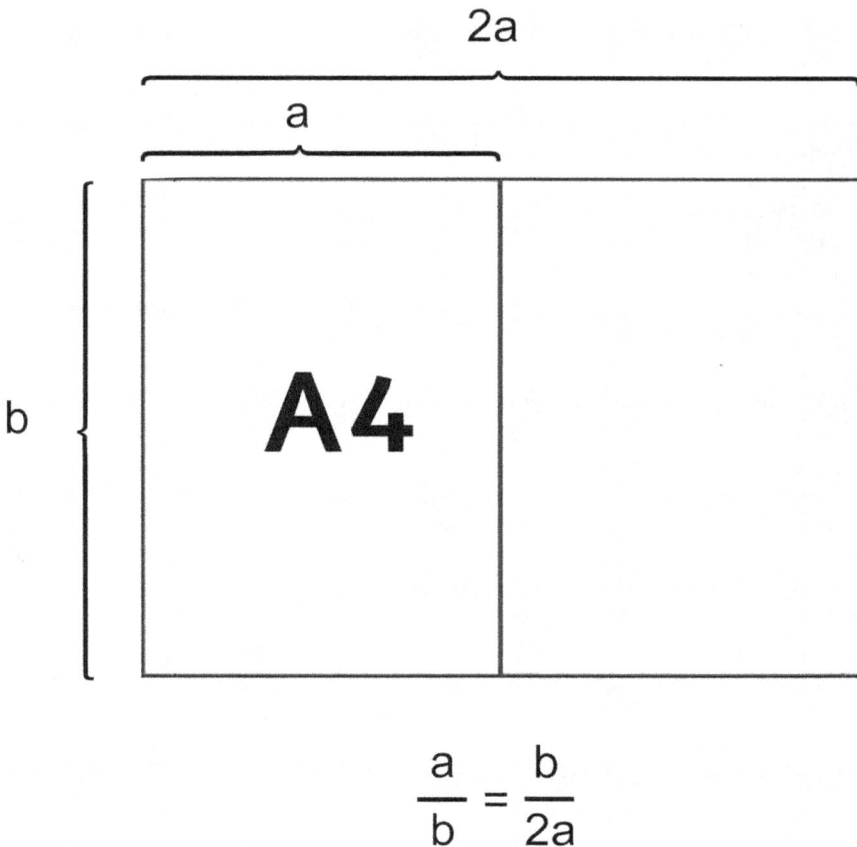

$$\frac{a}{b} = \frac{b}{2a}$$

Figure 6.8 An A4 page with the proportions of the golden ratio

Source: Illustration by the author

world: the ratio between a tree's stem and a branch of that tree is identical to that between the branch and a twig on that branch. If we now draw an analogy between the large part of the ratio and the subject, and the smaller part and the object, then by cutting the sheet in half, we switch the positions of the subject and the object. What hitherto was the object (the smaller part on the A3 sheet) turns into the subject (the big part on the A4 sheet). The golden ratio is an aesthetic principle embraced by artists and mathematicians alike, from Pythagoras and Phidias to Fibonacci (Meisner, 2018). As said, what happens in this world is never repeated. It is only when signifiers are attached to these events that iterability enters (the signifier can be repeated, creating an effect of things repeating themselves). The object is constituted by consistent repetition. In the case of the golden ratio, what is repeated is the proportions. This has an effect of harmony and serenity against the tense background of ever-changing reality, of our inability to predict what is to come. We witness a child's inflexibility when we tell that child a story again but omitting some details. Repetition loses its calming effect when it is not exact. The repetition of proportion is a complex variant of repetition, even if the elements take different roles on each iteration.

We can observe the conversion of container/contained relations between subject and object in the fable about the hunter and the monkey: the hunter finds a hollow tree trunk and places a nut in a small pit inside the trunk. When the monkey notices the nut, he reaches out for it, but his fist, now holding on to the nut, gets stuck when he wants to withdraw it. The hunter appears and captures the monkey. In grabbing the object, the monkey loses sight of the fact that he himself is an object (of the hunter). As a subject, the monkey takes hold (of the nut), and as an object, he is captured (by the hunter). When a patient talks to us about her objects, we as analysts will be looking out also for how she sees herself as an object. Similarly, if a child is a parent's object, a doll which the child plays with designates the child as a subject. When a child in treatment behaves unkindly toward a doll, the analyst can relate to the child as a subject. Then we will engage the child about the way he has chosen to treat the doll and about what such a treatment may entail. Things are different, however, if we respond to this behavior as if it were the child's way of talking about himself-as-an-object by means of the doll. We will empathize with his helplessness as an object. When he hits the doll, our response will be directed to his unconscious: "I understand that it hurts when they hit you". Even when the child refuses the interpretation and replies: "What do you mean, it's me who is hitting here", still the empathic message will resonate unconsciously. Another example is when a young child suffers from constipation due to psychological reasons, that is, she does not release her anal object. We might consider what the metaphor of constipation refers to: Could it be that the subject who does not release the object is the parents, who are trying too hard to control the child?

Lacan refers to three conditions that serve as metaphors for subject-object relations (Lacan, 1956–1957, Session 4, p. 112): the body part as object in the body as subject; the child as object in the mother as subject, and the partner as object in the relationship as subject. These metaphors can offer the basis for an inquiry into how a body symptom (relations between body and its parts or organs) reflects a child's relations with its parent, or the individual's participation in coupledom.

Opposite situations also occur, when the patient presents himself as though he were an object, while it is easy to observe how he makes his choices as a subject. This type of dialectic between subject and object positions is often present in the perverse personality structure.

Thus, the masochistic person pretends he is an object – "Hit me", he says to the sadist. "I don't want to", answers the sadist maliciously. While it is the subject who is asking to be beaten, the wanting, demanding subject – what he is asking for is to be treated as an object. We might reformulate the masochist's words like this: "Please set me free of the burden of being a subject, with his lack, by hitting me and treating me like a mere object". This disappoints the sadist because what he really wants is the victim's suffering to testify to his lack, as one of the key characteristics of the subject. And this he gets already in the form of the victim's frustration. The sadistic person wishes for the victim's suffering exactly to take possession of the object position for himself. The sadistic person, in other words, uses the other as his proxy, because like the masochistic person, the sadist too is trying to escape from a subject position.

The same occurs in other perversions too. The fetishistic person identifies with the thing; the necrophiliac attributes a soul to the other's dead body; and the sadist is controlled by a power that is greater than himself or herself, as in the earlier illustration of Eichmann who took pleasure in receiving orders from authority. When a voyeur looks at the body of a naked woman, we might easily assume it is her naked body that is his object. But if this were the case, then he could just as well take his pleasure from watching a woman who undresses

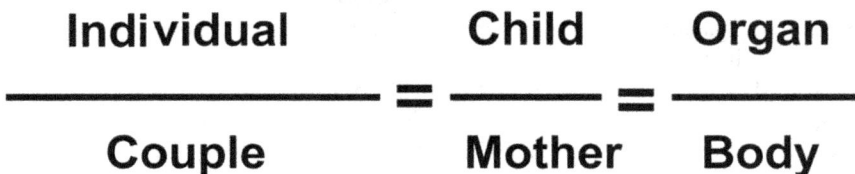

$$\frac{\text{Individual}}{\text{Couple}} = \frac{\text{Child}}{\text{Mother}} = \frac{\text{Organ}}{\text{Body}}$$

Figure 6.9 Analogy between three types of part-in-a-whole relations: individual as part of a couple, a child as part of a mother and an organ as part of a body

Source: Illustrative text by the author

herself while knowing she is being watched. His object, however, is her not-knowing that he is watching her. The voyeur asserts his subjecthood by being-in-the-know, in contrast with the victim of his voyeurism who doesn't know; the final aim, however, is to become an object through identification with the ignorance he projects on her. That is how he achieves his goal, which is to be an object.

It is in language that drive takes on a syntactic structure, like active, passive and reflective forms (in parallel to the active, passive and reflective voice in language). In the case of scopophilia, the active form is enacted by the one who looks; the passive form is occupied by the one who is being looked at, while the reflective is the one who puts himself or herself in the position of being looked at. Language acts on instinct (which is biological), transforming it into a drive that operates according to the rules of language. This is why talk has a healing function with symptoms – as far as they were created in language.

A couple came in for couple therapy because they were having frequent, violent fights. In their sexual practices, it transpired, there was a sadomasochistic element. Their conscious avoidance of this knowledge took the form of arguing about adjusting all sorts of practical arrangements between them, as though these aggressions were triggered by concrete reality (he didn't take out the garbage; she left dirty plates in the sink). Some frequently heard texts in this situation are: "Again I am the victim-object who has to take out the garbage instead of you". This is the therapist's interpretation: "Your sexual fantasy has really spun out of control", which suggests the existence of a subject seeking the pleasure of being absolved from subjecthood by turning into an object, a victim.

Lover and beloved

Commenting on Plato's *Symposium* in his seminar on transference (Lacan, 1960–1961, p. 1), Lacan describes the interchangeability of the roles, subject and object, in the case of love. Alcibiades takes the position of the lover, the subject, in relation to Socrates, who is the beloved, the object. What is the object attributed to Socrates, which arouses love? Socrates calls this mysterious object *agalma*. In Lacan's interpretation, this object is an empty box that holds another empty box, and so on – and deep down in the smallest box of all, nothingness is hiding. For Lacan, then, the subject is attractive, in the end, on account of what he or she lacks. Desire draws desire. The mechanism whereby lover and beloved switch roles, Lacan calls "the metaphor of love". When it turns out that the beloved one is loved due to *agalma*, in other words, because he has a lack, because he desires, he stands revealed as taking the position of the lover. Everything turns over, and the lover becomes the beloved. This dialectic explains many situations in love relationships, when the lover stops loving once he has gained or exposed the love of the beloved.

Over and beyond narcissistic explanations of the type "I will not join a club that accepts me as a member", this inversion has a structural component. When a person is in love, everybody falls in love with him. It is the *agalma* of his desire that attracts others. Once we accept the structural constraint that we cannot occupy both positions at once, it is easier to achieve a balanced love relationship; then we can understand a couple's arguments as an act of role switching. The quarrel starts when one side feels insufficiently loved and has been taking the role of the lover for too long. The guilty loved one tries to appease the angry lover; in doing so he takes on the role of the lover – until he too is fed up and kicks up a row. Another example is a patient who keeps finding partners who stop loving her. She wonders whether she surrenders too easily, loves too much, or maybe she should play hard to get. One possible interpretation is that she monopolizes the role of the lover, leaving no room for her partner to take that position. In other words, she needs to learn how to share.

Conscious and unconscious

In our clinical work, we aim, in due course, to see a reversal in the relations between conscious and unconscious. While at the start of the analysis, we tend to think of the unconscious as contained (my unconscious belongs to me), later it will come to be situated as a container (I belong to the unconscious). When the patient makes a mistake at the start of the treatment – say she turns left instead of right – that's what she'll see: a mistake. Her consciousness contains her mistakes. But when she repeats the same mistake, she will now interpret it, helped by the psychoanalyst, as a kind of Freudian slip. In other words, as a mistake of desire: "It was my unconscious that chose to turn left". Here the unconscious still belongs to the patient. "My" (as in "my unconscious") reflects a position of ownership of the unconscious, one in which consciousness includes the unconscious.

It is crucial to therapeutic progress that there should be a shift of identification from the conscious to the unconscious. The unconscious wish will be seen by the analysand as more fundamental, more exact with relation to the subject than the conscious wish of the figure the patient believes she is. The psychoanalyst will support this shift by urging the patient to continue associating in the direction of the mistake or slip, rather than return to the conscious plan to report on the past week's events. This involves a process so radical that even the word "mistake" is not quite appropriate. It is hard to accept that we are not the masters of our own house and that it's the unconscious who is in charge. As the analysis advances, the patient increasingly identifies with her unconscious choices, leading to an about-face at the end of the treatment. Now the conscious mind is contained in the unconscious. From this perspective, the patient will say: "I chose to turn left even though my conscious mind mistakenly thought to turn right".

One of psychoanalysis's basic principles regarding free association is "Say anything that comes to mind, no matter what". This is the way to circumvent the defenses of the unconscious censor. This is also why it's best to come to the session unprepared, to try and talk with as little control as possible. You can compare this to an adult and a child playing at odds and evens: the adult can easily predict the child's behavior. This is because the adult has a wider perspective; she can guess the child's thoughts better than the child can figure the adult's thoughts. The child's chances of winning at least some of the time are a function of her ability to act arbitrarily, that is, unpredictably. Free associations release the subject from the censor.

Chuang Tzu dreamed he was a butterfly (Lacan, 1978 [1963–1964], p. 76), and when he woke, he could not be sure if he was not the imaginary product of a butterfly dreaming, he was Chuang Tzu. He suggests an inside-out, paradoxical situation in which the (dreamed) butterfly contains or enfolds the (dreaming) person. And yes, we may well ask in what sense is he more of a butterfly than the human persona he recognizes as himself? Had Chuang Tzu been an analysand, we could have tried to clarify and interpret, for instance, as follows: the butterfly, in so far as it is a symbol of freedom, testifies more to your hidden and true desires than the desires you know about consciously. In doing so, however, we revert to Chuang Tzu himself who features as free in the metaphor of the butterfly. The more radical identification as a butterfly implies that no matter with what figure he identifies, whether it is the human body or the butterfly, it is always no more than a representation. Whether the persona is that of a human or of a butterfly, it meets the subject's need to adopt a form in order to identify with one.

When we animate and personify the unconscious mind and the censor using the word "want", we should remember it is only an allegory: in Lacan's approach, the unconscious is not an entity but an algorithm of knowledge operating by virtue of the signifiers' combinatorics without the mediation of a knower. This has important ethical and clinical implications. At the completion of analysis, now that the patient has acknowledged he isn't a unified, undivided creature and that he is not in control of his fate the way he professed, the resulting or remaining mode of being is that of an algorithm, a system that produces meaning from the conjunction of signifiers. By the end of his analysis, the subject is more aware of the illusory nature of absolute freedom encapsulated in the statement "If only you choose". This is how we may interpret it when Lacan says that at the end of analysis, the subject is a poem, rather than the poet being the subject (Lacan, 1978 [1963–1964], p. XIII).

The superego and the id

The superego pretends it's a saint whose function is to rein in drives; it achieves this by letting it be known how one should conduct oneself and when to feel guilty about one's drives. On a second look, however, the superego turns out to be an abusive and sadistic function. If we situate the superego on the cross-cap as a container that converts into a contained at the crossing of the intersecting line, then it is contained by a sadistic id rather than containing the id. This can explain the paradox of the suffering righteous (*Babylonian Talmud, Tractate Berachot* 7:1): the harder a person strives to follow the moral imperative, the more exposed she will be to guilt and the blows of the sadist. The sadistic drive – which is exactly that, a drive – cannot be satisfied; it is a need that has been eroticized by the signifier, and this precludes satisfaction. Hence it comes under the paradox "if he starves it, it's sated; if he sates it, it is hungry" – which is resolved when we refuse the assumption that the fetish is the object. Once we understand that the fetish is a signifier, then the signifier produces a desire, and it is desire that knows no satisfaction.

Submission to the superego has come to be known as moral masochism: here *jouissance* is generated by taking the part of the guilty masochist, *jouissance* derived from the very existence of the law (Lacan, 1992 [1959], p. 20]). Being subject to the law, which constrains *jouissance*, the masochistic individual expresses *jouissance* in giving voice to his suffering. Rather than forfeiting *jouissance*, he pays for it in the currency of suffering. Alternatively, he can derive his pleasure from naming the imaginary Other (who relieves him of his orphanhood); or even that punishment may serve as evidence of a pleasure-giving transgression. Either way, guilt signals *jouissance*.

References

Babylonian Talmud, Tractate Berachot 7:1.

Deleuze, G., & Guattari, F. (1983). *On the line*. Los Angeles, CA: Semiotext, Massachusetts Institute of Technology Press.

Freud, S. (2001 [1919]). The uncanny. In *The standard edition* (Vol. 17, pp. 237–240). London: Vintage.

Hadar, U. (2013). *Psychoanalysis and social involvement*. New York: Palgrave Macmillan.

Hohwy, J. (2013). *The predicative mind*. Oxford, UK: Oxford University Press.

Lacan, J. (1956–1957). *Seminar IV – The object relation* (C. Gallagher, Trans.). Unpublished manuscript, Session 4, p. 112.

Lacan, J. (1958–1059). *Seminar VI – Desire and its interpretation* (C. Gallagher, Trans.). Unpublished manuscript, p. 235.

Lacan, J. (1960–1961). *Seminar VIII – Transference* (C. Gallagher, Trans.). Unpublished manuscript, p. 1.

Lacan, J. (1966–1967). *Seminar IVX – Logic of Phantasm* (C. Gallagher, Trans.). Unpublished manuscript.

Lacan, J. (1975–1976). *Seminar XXIII – Joyce the Sinthome* (C. Gallagher, Trans.). Unpublished manuscript, Session I, p. 1.

Lacan, J. (1978 [1963–1964]). *The seminar of Jacques Lacan, Book XI: The four fundamental concepts of psychoanalysis*. New York: Norton, p. 76.

Lacan, J. (1992 [1959]). *The seminar of Jacques Lacan, Book VII: The ethics of psychoanalysis* (D. Porter, Trans.). New York: Norton, p. 20.

Lacan, J. (2002). Seminar on "The Purloined Letter". In B. Fink (Trans.), *Ecrits*. New York: Norton.

Lacan, J. (2002 [1964]). The subversion of the subject and the dialectic of desire in the Freudian unconscious. In B. Fink (Trans.), *Ecrits* (p. 713). New York: Norton.

Laurent, E., & Miller, J. A. (1989, January). The other who doesn't exist and his ethical committees. In R. Golan et al. (Eds.), *Almanac of psychoanalysis*. Jerusalem: Technosdar.

Meisner, G. (2018). *The golden ratio*. New York: Racepoint.

Rucker, R. (1984). *The fourth dimension: A guided tour of the higher universe*. Boston, MA: Houghton Mifflin. Retrieved from http://sajun.org/index.php/Cross-cap

Chapter 7

The dimension of time

Afterwardsness

We are used to relate to time in the physical world as having an irreversible vector. Once an egg breaks, it does not go back to being a whole, unbroken egg. As long as time is an axis along which we can move only in one direction – time is not a dimension, we have no degree of freedom about it (much like the height axis is irrelevant to anything occurring on the two axes of a two-dimensional plane). In the human world, the domain of language, time is reversible. In this chapter, I show how memory and writing, the rewriting of history, enable us to move in time and thereby live in a fourth dimension (the dimension of time).

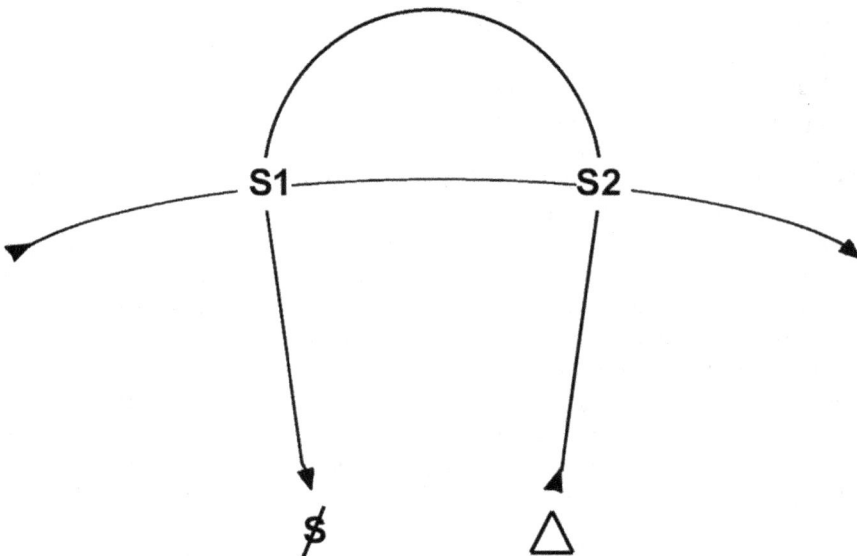

Figure 7.1 The graph of desire

Source: Illustration reproduced by the author

DOI: 10.4324/9781003232285-08

This simple graph of desire illustrates how the last word adjudicates the context and hence the meaning of the first word, in retrospect. On the diachronic axis, describing the sequence of words in their appearance in speech on the axis of time, the word S1 appears first (on the left), with the word S2 appearing further on. Take the statement "It turns" – S1 ("It") comes before S2 ("turns"). The figure, however, includes an additional axis, the synchronic axis, beginning down on the right and ending down on the left. The direction of this axis is counter to that of speech time. This axis takes off from the last word in the sentence (S2), deploying it as a context for the first word (S1). So, for instance, in the sentence "It turns when it works, the washing machine", the washing machine is the S2 which in retrospect determines what it was that turned at S1. The retrospective view, afterwardsness, solves several paradoxes. It illuminates transference relations and psychoanalytic interpretation, and it is crucial to the ethics of psychoanalysis, in the development of its theory and of the psychoanalyst's desire.

Interpretation

In his *Story* (McKee, 1997), Robert McKee argues that a story should surprise time and again, at the end of each and every sentence, paragraph, scene and so on. What else is a twist in the plot than the action of a second signifier which utterly changes the first signifier? When we listen to a patient, we wait for the word by means of which we will interpret what was said until now. This is our paradigmatic way of pointing at desire and *jouissance*, at the presence of the subject, and relate her or him to the desires she or he articulates.

A patient complains about grinding her teeth. This is how she describes the symptom: "When I catch myself grinding my teeth, I immediately relax, but then it returns". The word "catch", appearing after the actual teeth grinding is, in fact, the very reason for the teeth grinding. The symptom is a vicious cycle, so that its end ties into its beginning, with the word "catch" serving as the link between end and beginning. Mentioning her strong desire in relation to her work, the patient says that she's trying to catch up, with the utmost effort, with everything she must do but she cannot cope with all of it. If it was a concrete solution we were after, telling her to work less might be adequate. But this is not where her problem is located. It is linked to the fact that "catching hold with all her might" is somehow not legitimate. This statement, therefore, comes in the form of her jaws locking, or getting caught. The analytic investigation will probe the origin of this unlawfulness of desire. Similarly, a patient who says he suffers from tension says he must get a hold on this tension, master it. During the analysis, we discover his ambition to reach the very top, make big achievements, something he perceived as illicit. Again, here, the same "mastering", which appears in the context of his dealing with the resulting tension (he must master, get a hold, because of the tension symptom) converts into the reason for that tension, the repressed wish to master, achieve the utmost.

Emergence of the subject, unconscious and transference

The young mother, for fun, taught her 2-year-old to respond as follows, every time she says: "Mummy is . . ." – the little one responds: "gorgeous". Everybody who hears it smiles. Does he understand what he is saying? Of course not. Nor does he intend to make people laugh. As far as he is concerned, he has not been making a joke. But the fact of the laughter he evokes is psychically inscribed, in retrospect as a joke he told with the aim to amuse his audience. The evoked laughter comes to frame what he said as a joke. Having repeated it, this time with the intention to provoke mirth, he will eventually invent a narrative about the past in which he features as having aimed to provoke his audience's laughter right from the start. In other words, the one whose intention it was is the subject. There is no subject prior to the others' laughter. It is only after the fact of the audience's amusement that this subject is historically established in retrospect. The subject emerges when his or her existence is assumed by him or her in retrospect.

Similarly, the unconscious exists by the grace of its assumed existence. When we say to a patient: "Ah, that's a Freudian slip you made, that's your unconscious. Someone or something in your unconscious made this Freudian error, causing you to turn left rather than right", – we assume, when we say this, the existence of a subject of the unconscious who wishes something, intends something, behind those slips of the tongue and dreams. Like the child who becomes a subject with hindsight, who believed, in retrospect, that he had intentions – the unconscious, too, has no ontological status: it is not real. This is a radically ethical position. Like God or love, it is a conceptualization whose existence we wish for. We want patients to say "I have unconscious intentions", because it is in this manner that the subject of the unconscious is created. Freud, therefore, was not quite right in calling the unconscious a "discovery". The Lacanian position is that the unconscious desiring subject is assumed and thereby it arises. And that once it emerges, it produces desires without depending on others to be assumed. In treatment, especially during the initial phase, the objective is to discover/produce desires; to get the engine of desire to work.

The two-directional movement on the graph of desire (from S1 to S2, and from S2 to S1) also takes place between patient and analyst, from the perspective of the patient's fantasy. The patient, occupying position S1, directs her words to who is in position S2, the one who is assumed to know, the one who presumably reads our thoughts. Assuming knowledge is one of Lacan's definitions for transference. The patient says: "I dreamed about an old woman, you probably think it is my mother". By way of supporting the unconscious, the patient casts the analyst as being in possession of this knowledge. To believe in the existence of knowledge, the patient must believe that there is someone who knows. The analyst from her side needs to support this belief by way of being enigmatic. The patient uses the assumption "That's probably what the analyst thinks" to express her unconscious thought. What remains for the analyst to respond is "So you said. Then let's talk about your mother".

The knowledge ascribed to the analyst also has an erotic aspect. The statement ". . . you probably think it is my mother" enfolds the assumption, "You want to know about my dream, about my mother, about my unconscious". The psychoanalyst's desire for (the patient's) unconscious knowledge is a crucial asset to the analysis, desire being the desire of the other: the psychoanalyst infects the patient with this desire. If the patient "brings in" a dream to the analyst, this is thanks to the fact that her dreams are wanted.

Suffering as truth validation

"I suffer; therefore, I am not imagining it, therefore there's some truth here" – this is a variation on "I pinch myself, therefore I am not dreaming". In these two statements, suffering confirms in retrospect some phenomenon. It is a confirmation that comes in two registers: First, through the statement: "After all, I wouldn't willingly choose to suffer, so believe me, if I suffer, it's because of something real (as for myself, it also confirms to me that I am not lying)". Second, the confirmation is mediated by the statement "Just like suffering cannot be denied, because it is real like physical pain, truth, too is real".

Present produced as retrospective effect of the future: myths beyond death

Not wanting any identification with his drunken father (Lacan, 1975–1976, p. 16), James Joyce decided to create his own identity. He was determined to become a celebrated writer, whose books would be read everywhere, even taught at the universities. On the lines of afterwardsness, he believed that given his future rise to fame, he was therefore already, in the present, a person bound to become a great author – this belief gave him his identity. On the basis of his imagined and invented future, he retroactively derived the meaning of who he was in the present.

For psychoanalytic healing, the patient, too, projects herself and her analyst into a future fantasy when the analyst will have healed her. It may occur that the problem the patient wishes to treat does not allow for psychoanalytic work (e.g., a paranoid patient who mistrusts the analyst or one who is depressed and unable to leave his bed to come in for treatment). When this is the case, we face a paradoxical situation in which we must solve the problem to start treating it. This paradox is addressed in the transference relations. Something in the relations with the analyst produces a temporary respite, the problem is suspended: the patient has faith that things will be OK, that there is someone who has the knowledge needed to make for a better future. This situation forms a window of opportunity, reprieve in the form of what has been called a "flight into health" – enabling to start the work of analysis even if this opening is only temporary.

When her brothers were killed, Antigone insisted on burying them against the king's decree. She knew that she risked being put to death herself (Lacan, 1992 [1959–1960]). Antigone was the daughter of Oedipus who had transgressed against the most fundamental laws of the family. In acting as she did, Antigone took it upon herself to rehabilitate the laws of the family according to the following logic:

> If I die not having honored the laws of the family, my life, with hindsight, will have lost all value. If I am willing to honor them, even at the risk of my life, I know that I will have lived a life worth living.

Certain myths that deal with the future also make possible faith in immortality. Freud's notion of the death drive can be considered one of these. The death drive, according to him, is the drive of anything living to return to its previous state of inertia (Freud, 2001 [1920], p. 3), as in "for dust thou art, and unto dust shalt thou return". Freud, however, takes an animistic approach when he attributes to physical entropy the wish of dust to return to itself, as though inert matter had mind and will. Identifying with the inanimate matter that will remain after his living body disintegrates, Freud buys himself immortality.

From Lacan's myth of the lamella too (Lacan, 1977 [1963–1964], p. 183), immortality can be derived. The lamella is a Lacanian invention, referring to a mythological creature, monocellular and amoeba-like, which reproduces asexually by doubling itself. It has no gender and does not die. Sexuality and death are always inextricable (in sexual creatures). This asexual, monocellular being symbolizes the thing that does not die. The lamella is Lacan's metaphor for the signifier. The identification of the subject with the nonliving and therefore non-dying signifiers is her gate to eternity. When we identify with the word, therefore, we obtain a window unto what is beyond our biological time on earth, an eternal existence that resembles that of the monocellular creature.

When Hamlet asks, "To be or not to be?" another question arises: To be what? Hamlet has been ordered to kill his uncle who killed his father – but he doesn't obey. For Lacan, Hamlet is the first neurotic man. Unlike Antigone, he does not act in the service of his father; he fails to stick to the mission of his family. It is only at the very end, having been grazed by the poisoned sword and realizing these are his final moments, that he acts. "To be" is to be as a desiring subject, to uphold the symbolic order that upholds us as subjects, even at the price of biological death.

The absence of *points de capiton*

If significance is to be determined (of a word, for instance, or of a statement), there must exist what Lacan called *points de capiton* (Lacan, 1988 [1954], p. 183), – anchoring points – between S1 and S2, between signifier and signified. These are like the buttons which the mattress maker sews onto the mattress at certain points, so as to fasten the textile on both sides through the soft filling. One function of cutting a session serves this purpose of *point de capiton* or making meaning, like the period at the end of the sentence. In the absence of S2, meaning is postponed to the future, again and again. This condition can be observed in phenomena of infinite *jouissance*, like addiction or hyper-abundant production of meaning, as in empty, unbounded or uninhibited chatter, behaviors which are bound to cause much suffering.

From a phantasmatic perspective the just-one-more, which for instance the child begs for, this one more will bring gratification. There is, however, clearly no way to really satisfy the child. A residual lack always remains. It is hence "more" as such that is the object (rather than the object he is asking more of). In his seminar *Encore* (more), (Lacan, 1998 [1972–1973]), Lacan develops the idea of a different *jouissance*, namely, the *jouissance* of non-satisfaction, of the object of the anorexic person, of nothing. If the partners in a relationship believe that each can fill this lack in the other, then the relationship, which cannot sustain such an expectation, will come to an end. It was only when a patient finally talked about the pain of her existence without reference to her marital situation, that work on that relationship became possible. Sharing this pain with her partner, she changed her position: rather than demanding he should supply whatever would make her whole, she communicated her lack. Lacan sees this as the basis for love: one gives what one hasn't (Lacan, 1965–1966, p. 218).

References

Freud, S. (2001 [1920]). Beyond the pleasure principle. In J. Strachey (Trans.), *The standard edition* (Vol. 18). London: Vintage.

Lacan, J. (1965–1966). *Seminar XIII – The object of psychoanalysis* (C. Gallagher, Trans.). Unpublished manuscript.

Lacan, J. (1975–1976). *Seminar XXIII – Joyce the Sinthome* (C. Gallagher, Trans.). Unpublished manuscript.

Lacan, J. (1977 [1963–1964]). *The seminar of Jacques Lacan, Book XI: The four fundamental concepts of psychoanalysis*. New York: Norton.

Lacan, J. (1988 [1954]). *The seminars of Jacques Lacan, Book II: The ego in Freud's theory and in the technique of psychoanalysis*. New York: Norton.

Lacan, J. (1992 [1959–1960]). *The seminar of Jacques Lacan, Book VII: The ethics of psychoanalysis*. New York: Norton.

Lacan, J. (1998 [1972–1973]). *Encore – On feminine sexuality – The limits of love and knowledge: Book XX*. New York: Norton.

McKee, R. (1997). *Story: Substance, structure, style and the principles of screenwriting*. New York: HarperCollins.

Chapter 8

The paradox of the act

A patient speaks again and again about how unhappy he is with his wife and why he wants to separate from her. It seems he is building up the file which will eventually allow him, in his inner courthouse, to go free. He struggles with guilt vis-à-vis the children, with "what will the neighbors say", with his financial worries – but though he finds solutions to each of these concerns, he still does not make the step. How much more evidence against her will it take until he can make the decision? What will tip the scales? But the metaphor of the scales doesn't really work here. What it takes is an act.

Another patient suffers from vaginismus each time sexual intercourse is on the cards. She too avoids doing an act. The act is a paradoxical deed in which the subject engages in something that radically changes her. The more the first patient defines himself in terms of his being married, the more radical a change will a divorce be – to the point of altering his very identity. The second patient has a hard time making the transition from what she perceives as being a virgin to being a woman, an act which will turn her into a different subject. As said, in the case of giving up tobacco smoking, the main obstacle often is neither nicotine dependency nor addiction as such but the shift in identity from smoker to nonsmoker. Why are such changes so threatening? Because during the act itself, when the subject is already no longer who she was and still not who she will be, the subject disappears (until when she comes out the other end of the act and reconstructs the moment of her creation). This necessary vanishing of the subject in the act is the reverse side of the principle according to which desire creates the reality in which it occurs. A patient complains he has no desire or that his desire is inhibited for reasons he does not understand. At the same time, he speaks scornfully of people who naively believe all kinds of things are important. Ever since his mother died when he was a young boy, he insists life is meaningless.

> How are you supposed to feel desire if you make short shrift of any meaning-giving myth? How will you have a mission, a purpose, take meaningful action, if you are unwilling to support a story that supports you as a character in a narrative with a plot?

DOI: 10.4324/9781003232285-09

He responded that it was all make-believe, on which I asked him: "But how will you make anything of anything if you don't make your belief?"

Lacan advises the psychoanalyst not to deny the virtual nature of symbolic existence, on the one hand, but also not to refuse participating in the one game that allows a person to experience desire (Lacan, 1973–1974). The desire for myth makes it possible for desire to exist within the myth – it is like a person lifting himself up by his collar.

But if the act belongs to the subject, why does it fall to the psychoanalyst to cut the session? If the patient has been saying something that exhausts the point at hand, that constitutes a decisive moment, or a definitive statement like "That's it!" – then cutting the meeting at that point is an act of the patient's unconscious . . . as the analyst interprets it. It is the patient's unconscious who is the master who decides – the psychoanalyst acts like its servant by making room for it.

References

Lacan, J. (1973–1974). *Seminar XXI – Les Non-Dupes Errent* (C. Gallagher, Trans.). Unpublished manuscript.

Chapter 9

Paradoxes without a solution

Meaning emerges from putting words together. Each word that is added to or taken away from a sentence changes its meaning: this is how interpretation operates. Interpretation may come in the form of a word the psychoanalyst adds, or when the patient stops in mid-sentence omitting some words he was going to say. The symbolic unconscious is structured like a language, a contextual system that produces meaning by putting words together. The real unconscious, by contrast, is made up of unconnected words, like signs or proper names lacking in context and therefore lacking in meaning. A word heard in childhood is likely to enfold both excitement and pain (*jouissance*) and to persistently produce suffering, without the possibility of replacing its meaning with another one. The psychoanalyst, in such cases, is helpless, robbed of the interpretive tools he knows how to wield. In the introduction to the English edition of *The Four Fundamental Concepts of Psychoanalysis* (Lacan, 1978 [1963], p. 250), Lacan refers to the Real unconscious as being located outside the truth because it does not include meanings that are either true or false: "When the space of a lapsus no longer carries any meaning (or interpretation), then only is one sure that one is in the [Real] unconscious. One knows". One possible interpretation of these words is that the Real cannot be inserted into a symbolic system in which meanings can alter depending on interpretation, by means of the mechanisms of metaphor and metonymy. Transformations cannot be deployed on the Real. It stays intact and impenetrable to change. No fetishization of sexual energy can be achieved, and no diagnosis is possible of the body's murmurings, when they are the isolated signifiers of the Real unconscious. There are pains that cannot be removed by changes of perspective, when we open our field of vision into a broader context, or by shifting to another dimension in which a paradox responsible for psychic pain is undone. None of these logical actions pertain to the Real unconscious.

The logical maneuver I have been elaborating here, that of solving a paradox, works on the assumption that the symptom is meaningful. A paradox without a solution can be one of two things: either it does have a meaning which is yet to be discovered, or it has none. These two possibilities are not easily discerned. Typically, a paradox will manifest itself as impossible exactly until a solution

DOI: 10.4324/9781003232285-10

presents itself. Once a solution presents itself in the clinic, it can be formulated as a bit of theory. Where no solution is found, the assured knowledge of there being no symbolic solution becomes a potential solution. In such a case, acceptance of the impossible may alleviate the sense of impotence and failure. Even after the meanings of the symptom have been released in the form of a narrative, the real core of *jouissance* goes on sustaining the symptom. Interpretation has a limited capacity to reduce suffering, and at this point all there is left is for the patient to choose whether one lives with this *jouissance* or gives up on it, in so far as this is possible.

In "Beyond the Pleasure Principle" (Freud, 2001 [1920]), Freud explains how the human creature (Lacan will say: the speaking creature) takes pleasure from tension. Thus, anxiety can be of the kind that will be helped by release or discharge of meaning or, conversely, by ascribing meaning; it can, however, also be associated with something real like the fear of death – for which we cannot offer an alternative story. Then, what is left is the possibility to act.

In the case of paranoid delusion, meaning will tend to be attributed in terms of the other's desire to enjoy at the subject's expense, often by ascribing significance to phenomena, including arbitrary ones. Here the psychoanalyst's ability to stay outside that significance, that is, to tolerate the experience of meaninglessness, is valuable in the work with psychotic patients. This position will later be a resource at the post-psychotic stage when patients emerge from delusional meaning. It will enable the psychoanalyst to offer comfort and extend sympathy for the loss of the meaning-making delusion.

Regarding neurotic structures, patients presenting with anxiety can also be treated by stitching together historical myths that explain the origins of the anxiety, with which wishes of and identifications with others it allies itself. In this manner, a myth evolves that soothes the anxiety arising from meaninglessness. That is what a paradoxical solution aims for. Another more ambitious type of treatment aims at accepting the meaninglessness of the unresolved paradox. In this case, the point, rather than finding a narrative to live in, is for the subject to agree to be, to some extent, outside the narrative. Agreement of this kind is key to an analysis which is also a form of training to be an analyst.

Paradox showed Freud the way to the unconscious, and to this day, it is a source of psychoanalytic development. Psychoanalysis may go in the footsteps of physics, which by evolving quantum theory has already adjusted itself to the failure of a logical Newtonian model to predict the behavior of subatomic particles. In psychoanalysis, too, we encounter phenomena that do not yield to deterministic-historical interpretation or to structural interpretations that suggest the strategies constitutive of reality and desire. This is the domain of the Real unconscious (Soler, 2018), where logic or meaning is not to be found. Some signifiers exist unsupported by the logical structure which would make it possible to effect change and conversions of meaning. Some signifiers, seared into consciousness, are saturated by *jouissance*, and that's it.

References

Freud, S. (2001 [1920]). Beyond the pleasure principle. In *The standard edition* (Vol. 18). London: Vintage.

Lacan, J. (1978 [1963]). *The seminar of Jacques Lacan Book XI – The four fundamental concepts of psychoanalysis*. New York: Norton, p. 250.

Soler, C. (2018). *Lacan – The unconscious reinvented* (E. Faye & S. Schwartz, Trans.). London & New York: Routledge.

Index

Page numbers in *italics* refer to Figures.

For Product Safety Concerns and Information please contact our EU
representative GPSR@taylorandfrancis.com
Taylor & Francis Verlag GmbH, Kaufingerstraße 24, 80331 München, Germany

9 7 8 1 0 3 2 1 4 0 8 4 1